W9-BCT-716

Risen Life

JOHN E. COCKAYNE, JR.

Risen Life

Healing a Broken World

Joseph G. Donders

ORBIS BOOKS

Maryknoll, New York 10545

The Catholic Foreign Mission Society of America (Maryknoll) recruits and trains people for overseas missionary service. Through Orbis Books, Maryknoll aims to foster the international dialogue that is essential to mission. The books published, however, reflect the opinions of their authors and are not meant to represent the official position of the society.

Copyright © 1990 by Joseph G. Donders
Published by Orbis Books, Maryknoll NY 10545
All rights reserved
Manufactured in the United States of America

Library of Congress Cataloging-in-Publication Data

Donders, Joseph G.
  Risen life: healing a broken world / Joseph G. Donders.
    p.   cm.
  Includes bibliographical references.
  ISBN 0-88344-688-X (pbk.)
  1. Spiritual life—Catholic authors.   2. Church and the world.
3. Liberation theology.   4. Sociology, Christian (Catholic)
5. Catholic Church—Doctrines.   I. Title.
BX2350.2.D639   1990
248.4'82—dc20
                                                    90-47168
                                                    CIP

Contents

Introduction

A Recurring Question

In recent years I have frequently encountered an advertisement for a new religious journal. It is a bold ad that catches the eye. The text begins, "In many circles the myth still circulates that religion is the preserve of the dimwitted and unlettered." It then proceeds to quote an article from the *New York Times Magazine* on the "return to religion" among intellectuals and an "undeniable renewal of interest in religion."

There are signs of a renewed interest in religion. Even the classical religious story told in the West is selling better than ever. The United Bible Society sold sixteen million Bibles and thirteen million copies of the New Testament in 1989. This is an increase of more than 1.5 million copies over the previous year.

Certainly many people are willing to plug into the spirit and the energy of those books. But still difficulties remain. Everyone with growing children in our Western world—whether in Europe, Australia, or North America—knows about one of those difficulties. You can see it when you look around in church on a Sunday morning. The bored expression on children's faces makes it clear just how much interest they have in religion!

Why is it that the new generation is no longer fascinated

by that which was the inspiration and life of their grandparents? How often have I heard parents ask, "Where did we go wrong? Were we too lenient? Were we too strict?" But such questions don't really get to the real problem.

How are we to answer a child who asks, "Why should I go to church? It doesn't mean a thing to me." Surely we have all encountered the question — if not from our own children or grandchildren, then from friends. Certainly a large percentage of Western Christians go to church — if at all — simply because they are accustomed to it. If that is the case, none of them would be able to convince others that this is a sufficient reason to join them. But even the issues that were so compelling for earlier generations, issues to which our faith once responded — sin, guilt, personal redemption — seem to fade away in the light of today's problems: the possibility of nuclear disaster, questions of economic, social, and ecological crisis that threaten human survival.

No wonder that we are continually faced by that ever-recurring question. It is posed to me quite often by very different people in different places and circumstances. Sometimes the question is raised after a glass of good wine among friends; at other times, in the harsh glare of a television studio, in a sunlit street in Cardiff, in a car driving through Australia's endless plains, or in front of a fire late in the evening, high in the East African mountains.

"Why do you remain so intrigued by that man Jesus? Why don't you let him go? Do you really need him?" Sometimes the question is phrased in other ways: "Why do you remain a Christian? Why do you remain a member of the Roman Catholic Church?"

Those who raise the question have often answered it for themselves. They have left the church and with it perhaps all organized religion behind. It is not an easy question to answer. And yet answer it I must, for ultimately the question is one I pose to myself.

I have arrived at an age when looking back definitely opens

a wider perspective on the world and time than looking forward. Most of my life has been concerned with Jesus and the church. I have published scores of articles, almost a thousand published sermons, and over fifty books and booklets. I have given countless talks, taught in several continents, and participated in radio and television programs all over the world.

A cynical reader might suppose that this was the only way I could make a living. Such a remark only makes the question more difficult to answer. It suggests that I may not even have acted in good faith, that I am either deceiving myself or deceiving others. And maybe both.

All the more reason to find an answer.

Yet I wonder whether it is really possible to formulate a single answer once and for all. Once you have found the complete answer you are finished; you have come to the end of your story. You no longer have ideas, but the ideas have you. Having arrived at the full answer, you become the prisoner of your own response. It is those who know all the answers who cause the most mischief in human history.

From my teaching years in Europe and Africa, I remember how the students were never satisfied with a victory over the university administration or the faculty. Their first reaction was always the same: *The struggle continues*. They were right.

And it seems to me that in that slogan there is the beginning of an answer. The struggle continues. Every reply poses a new question. Every structure has to be outgrown. Every solution has to be transcended. No situation should encircle and capture us to such an extent that we are unable to seek a wider truth. No fixed abode should arrest our search. No answer can be the final one.

At this point both friend and critic interpose: "Then what about the church you belong to? Why stick with it and with its pretensions of knowing all—what is more, of knowing it infallibly?"

I will confess: Often I do have difficulties.

One day, while visiting my family in Europe I brought a

set of stickers for my godchild. I had been to a novelty shop in a shopping mall and had bought all the stickers I could find: teddy bears, unicorns, flowers, animals, stars, even Garfield and Snoopy. One set represented religious sayings like "God loves you." It was interesting to see the spontaneous reaction of that young teenager. She admired all the sets, especially the unicorns, but when she saw the religious one she sighed, "What a bore!," and put it aside.

My trouble is that I can understand why she said that. While the teddy bears and unicorns sparked her imagination and responded to all kinds of needs, the religious imagery fell flat. It didn't just fail to meet a response — there was more in her remark than mere boredom. She was downright suspicious; she didn't trust it.

It would be an exaggeration to say that she knew, at her age, that what the church has to offer would be irrelevant to her life and her world. Yet she must have felt something like that. And I must admit that she is not the only one.

I can empathize with her position, as I do with the many teenagers I have to confront in church on a Sunday morning, their faces straight and their eyes without a twinkle of light. I think I can empathize with all those who have left the church — not because they were against Jesus, but because of something else, because they so seldom experienced Jesus to be alive in his church.

A friend told me about her sixteen-year-old son. She could not convince him to come to church with her. It did not mean anything to him, he said. And yet she found the New Testament next to his bed with a highlighter in it. Jesus fascinated him; the church did not.

I myself have no difficulty with Jesus. He is the most fascinating person I ever met in my life. The difficulty is elsewhere. It is admitting that I belong to the group around Jesus that sometimes bothers me.

It is difficult to explain what I mean. Let me try to do so by using the example of someone else. She is a Jewish mystic.

Her name is Simone Weil. In 1938 she wrote that Christ himself came down and took possession of her. Her priest friends advised her to consider baptism because of this mystical experience. After much reflection and prayer her answer was that she preferred not to be baptized. For her, that would mean belonging to an institutional structure. And she could not visualize belonging in the name of Jesus to a group that would exclude others, a group that would break bread only among "insiders" but not with "outsiders." It was as if life were given not to be lived, energy were to be stored but not used.

In our day and age it has become more difficult than ever to belong to any exclusive group, even if that group is the church. Yet, this exclusivism is only one reason why the church in its teaching, its doctrines, and its rites often seems irrelevant to our world.

So the question recurs: Why remain?

I remain because the Catholic church — notwithstanding all its historic failures — remains the keeper of the pearl of which Jesus spoke, the channel of the kingdom energy which he sparked in this world. It is in the church that the treasure is revealed, though yet it remains hidden. It is there and it is not yet there. It is given and not given. It is old, though it must be both old and new. It is a house that offers safety, divine and human company and comfort, that often limits and restricts the energy and life it contains, but then again bursts out in new life.

I remain in the church beause it is through her that I first came into contact with the Spirit that enlivens both me and the world. I remain in the church because it is my only hope.

There is, among the sacred books of the Bible, one author in particular who faced the same problems that confront us and who, in his time, made a similar discovery. His name is Luke.

Luke describes enthusiastically the power and energy he encountered in the early Christian communities. In these communities women and men did not just sit down and worship to save their souls in a world that was corrupt and beyond hope, but instead, under the influence of the Spirit, set about to organize solutions to the problems they faced.

Luke repeats the story of Jesus for a new and modern public, most probably living in Rome. While remaining loyal to Jesus' vision, he transplants the gospel from its Judaic and Palestinian setting into a new, wider, and some would say more corrupt world. He depicts Jesus from the beginning of his appearance as a healer in Nazareth against the backdrop of a world that is sick and dying. Then as now the question was asked: Why belong to the church? Luke's gospel is written from the point of view of persons who might answer this question by pointing to themselves: Don't you see in us the fire that is cauterizing the wounds of this world? Don't you notice in us what the Spirit can do in you?

Luke never personally encountered Jesus. Instead, he encountered Jesus in the Christian church. In this sense he is nearer to us today than were the original disciples. For that reason he is a valuable guide.

In the beginning of his Gospel Luke explains that he felt a pastoral need to recount the story of Jesus. Luke wrote for the well-to-do, emancipated and sophisticated women and men in the "First World" of his time. He presents Jesus as the type of person they could recognize and identify with.

In Luke's approach Jesus is a healer in whose presence people—and the communities they form—may discover in themselves the spiritual and physical powers needed to heal themselves and the world in which they live.

Unencumbered by all kinds of symbols and technical language, Luke touches in his Jesus story a nerve that is recognizably ours, and empowers us to undertake what all of us—young and old—are hoping for: the healing of our broken world.

Chapter One

Between Old and New

Whenever we are asked to explain what Jesus or the church mean to us, we can only answer with the story of our own experience. There is no other way.

It is not a matter of witnessing, which suggests that we have something to prove. The witnessing that goes on in so many church meetings often has just that suspect quality. It smacks of propaganda or advertising. Witnessing wants to force an issue, to provoke an engagement. It is one's own personal story that is intriguing.

If I am asked, "Do you honestly think and feel that there is something real in your faith, that you have touched life?" my honest answer is "yes." That "yes" is the story of my own life.

I was born and raised in the Netherlands in a part of the country that was predominantly Catholic and relatively poor. Very early in life I developed a missionary vocation. It began with my grandmother, who subscribed to a number of mission journals. Once a month I was allowed to come and collect them from her. With glowing heart and burning ears I read the stories of far-off lands. Evenings would find me hiding under the table with my precious journals, not to be discovered and sent to bed before I had finished reading them.

The theology of those journals was simple. All those who

had not heard of Jesus were lost. This fact was underscored by the accompanying pictures: the people were half-naked. Clearly, they had not heard about Jesus Christ; clearly, they were doomed. But the articles told readers how to free these lost souls. If you sent in some money a missionary would take care that one of them would be liberated from the captivity of the devil. She or he would be baptized, and the new Christian would receive the name you chose!

I decided on a more radical approach. I would become a missionary myself.

One day the parish priest asked those of us preparing for first Communion who among us would like to become a priest. I raised my hand, but I was not alone. Quite a few hands went up. Then he asked how many would like to become missionaries. This time only a few hands were raised. One of them was mine.

(To be honest, I don't think my vocation was fostered by pure altruism. I will admit that I longed to see something more of the world than my grandparents and parents had seen.)

One day I heard in my parish a sermon by a missionary who was returning to Africa on the coming Friday. There was, of course, a collection for him and his mission. I had only the three cents my mother had given me for the three collections: one cent for each. I put them all in the bag for the missionary. But I wanted to give more. I remembered my savings at home — 65 cents in all, the fruit of some concerted effort. When I got home I took all that money and brought it to the address of the missionary. Since he wasn't at home, I gave the money to his mother and explained why I had come. With tears in her eyes, she said something I never forgot: "God must love you!"

I did not tell anyone. The following Saturday evening my mother was reading the local church paper. Suddenly, she looked up at me and said, "Here, listen to this. It might teach you something." It was a letter from the missionary thanking the parishioners for their generosity and expressing special thanks to that boy who had brought him all his savings (65 cents). "Now that is a boy!" said my mother. When I told her it was I she put down her paper, took off her glasses, and gave me a great hug.

In later years I often thought back on that moment, wondering what went on in me and in all those others around me who shared similar experiences. It is amazing how one can have, as a child, spiritual experiences that profoundly affect the whole of one's life. What is that energy that makes you forget about yourself, and that is, at the same time, so deeply self-gratifying?

The Second World War interrupted my plans, as it did the plans of everyone in the western world. As my parents wanted to keep their children together during that terrible time, I did not go to a junior seminary but to the local secondary school. That the war would interfere with much more than my plans, that the entire world as we knew it was going to change, none of us in that provincial, insulated Roman Catholic world could suspect.

But as children we were quite excited by the outbreak of war. Finally, we thought, some adventure was going to enter our quiet lives. Such feelings quickly passed. On May 13, 1940 we were playing outside in the garden behind our house when the German Air Force bombed the railway station only a few blocks from my home. At first the bombs looked like eggs falling out of the planes. I still remember how we pretended to fire enthusiastically at the planes with our sticks, changed into anti-aircraft guns. Almost immediately we heard the explosions and ran inside. Already, on that third day of the war, I lost some of my classmates.

The war was a horror, not only because of the fighting, but because of the consequent famine. For almost three years afterwards I had to remain in bed, recovering from the effects of starvation.

When it was over, I went to study to become a missionary

priest. I chose the major seminary of the Missionaries of Africa—then better known as the White Fathers, on account of their rather fancy arabic white dress, completed with a red fez.

It is, of course, unfair to judge such a seminary on the basis of our present perspective. Yet, I think it is fair to say that there was an almost totalitarian aspect to the organization of this institution. We were treated like children, intellectual activity was minimal, uniformity in all things was rigidly imposed.

I could say the same thing in more philosophical terms. It was an "essentialist" environment. Everything had been settled. The "essence" of everything was known. If you wanted to become a missionary the recipe was the same for everyone. All questions were answered, even before we asked them. One knew how we should dress, how we should pray, sleep, eat—the works. Naturally, we had our complaints. And yet we were remarkably uncritical of the underlying assumptions. It seemed even to us that this was how it should be.

It was such a consoling thought, one said, that the Superior General knew that all the White Fathers arose from their beds at the same time—5:30 A.M. in the summer, 6:50 A.M. in the winter. I too was consoled by this, though in retrospect it is hard to remember why. We changed from wool to cotton and from cotton to wool on the very same day, a routine that was independent of the actual weather or temperature. And what is more, we all believed exactly the same things in exactly the same way. Maybe that was only the ideal. But our theology manuals indicated just how we had to adhere—with what degree of certainty—to the different articles of our faith. The degree of evil attaching to each sin had been determined almost before it had ever been committed.

As I think of it now, it seems that we were trapped, caught in our own certainty. But of course at the time I had no such feelings. Although I may now portray those times as frightful, that is not how it seemed then. On the contrary, our lives were quite joyful and inspired.

We had all come together in our compassion for the Africans. We were united in our love for these distant people. And we shared in Christ's love. We prayed, studied, worked in the garden, walked endless walks in our free time, studied foreign languages, peeled and ate buckets of potatoes, lived a sober life, and were quite willing to overlook any hardship in view of God's Reign. In a way we formed a kind of church group within the Church.

As a philosophy student, that is to say, as someone who tried to understand his Latin textbooks, I became a member of a priest-students' union. It was called Vindicamus, a rather ambiguous name. It meant something like "we shall overcome," or "you will definitely hear from us."

The union had its origins in the Second World War. Back then local organizations had sprung up to support the seminarians, after the schools and colleges were forced to close. Our superiors did not exactly like the idea of a students' union, but they did not oppose it. We did something, however, they had probably not expected. At our annual meetings we started to read the Bible. In doing so, we made a discovery—a very simple discovery, that nevertheless changed our lives. Reading the Bible we discovered that Jesus related to different people in different ways.

We discovered the force and the power of the "encounters," the "meetings," the "I-Thou" relationship in the stories about him: the Samaritan woman, the Syro-Phoenician woman, Martha, Mary, Mary of Magdala, the widow of Nain, Peter and James, the Roman officer, Nicodemus—each one of them special, unique. Jesus did not approach all these persons with the same ready-made formula. He treated them all differently, respecting them equally as persons, but respecting also their personal gifts, needs, and destinies.

I still remember how enthusiastic we were at this discovery. I can describe this discovery, too, in more philosophical and technical language. We started to think "existentially."

A type of personalistic thinking had originated after the

Second World War in reaction to the Nazi attitude of blind obedience. You could not excuse yourself by stating that you were just following orders. You were responsible for your deeds. This discovery had profound implications for all of us. Every subsequent change in my life — and there have been many changes — has been rooted in and enabled by this fundamental shift in my thinking.

Some call it empowerment. Others call it the discovery of our own personal "giftedness." It might even be called "being reborn." Whatever you call it, for me it has remained the most fundamental change. But there were more to come.

In my last year of studies in Scotland, where I was ordained a priest in 1957, I read an article about Teilhard de Chardin, who had died in New York some time before. I was so intrigued by the article that I immediately ordered his book, *The Phenomenon of Man.* It was there, during a winter in Scotland, that I read his synthesis of natural history. And I did something I had not done since I was a small boy. After the lights went out, I remained with a flashlight at my table, reading with glowing heart and burning ears. I was fascinated. A whole new world was unfolding in my mind and heart.

Teilhard showed how the personalized world I had discovered was not the last step in human development. There was that other sphere in which all personalized human individuals were drawn together to the center of all things. Teilhard did not always call that center God; he spoke of it as the Omega Point. It was as if suddenly everything fell into place; science and spirituality could be combined, natural history and salvation history could be related to each other, the whole of humanity, the whole world, the whole of the universe was taken up in one powerful surging wave of energy and love.

I was not only struck by Teilhard's scientific and theological reflections, but also by the mystical experience communicated in his vision. He tells a story — it is not entirely clear whether it is his own experience or another's — about how a

French soldier once knelt in front of a consecrated host in a small village. As he looked at the exposed host it began to change, taking on all kinds of colors and forms, until finally he saw before him the whole of warring humanity, interlocked together in the reality of Christ. As I read this I could feel a whole new world unfolding in my heart and mind.

Again my life took a definite turn. Appointed for doctoral studies in philosophy at the Gregorian in Rome, I registered my intention to do my thesis on Teilhard's idea of evolution. My application was approved and accepted. I even started working on it, assembling the volumes I would be studying and the available commentaries. But at this point I was asked by my supervisors to suspend my project. The reading of Teilhard's works had been formally forbidden by the Vatican and his books were banned from seminary libraries.

It was a hard initiation into the way the church tries to keep its balance while facing a world and a humanity that is ever more coming into its own. All this was during the reign of Pope Pius XII. A short time later I walked in his funeral procession, little realizing that we were burying much more than a pope.

His successor, Pope John XXIII, was a man of advanced years, but sufficiently sensitive to the new winds blowing in the world that he convoked the Second Vatican Council. I was still in Rome at the time, and I remember the occasion, though I could not foresee the consequences. Pope John XXIII wanted to update the old essentialist structures of the church with the help of the new personalist and existentialist perspectives.

In the course of the Council a vigorous debate was waged between those who favored the classical essentialist approach and those who were influenced by the existential tendency. Neither side was the clear victor. The documents of Vatican II bear the influence of both perspectives. In the document on the church, *Lumen Gentium*, for example, we find the church described on the one hand as the People of God, but at the same time with a stress on the hierarchical, pyramidic structure. On the religious life, there are statements that all Christians are called to the same perfection, while others single out the professed religious life as an ideal above the rest. Mission is described as a dialogue that respects others in their religious freedom and tradition, but in other documents it is identified with seeking conversion.

Maybe it is a good thing that neither of the two sides won. It kept the tension alive. It did not close the dialogue between the new world and the everlasting vision, between the old church and the new believer.

It is at that intersection between faithfulness to the old and openness to the new that the hierarchically organized church interacts with a newly empowered membership. The church has difficulties with this new reality, but so has this new humanity with the church. It is at this cutting edge that our own faithfulness and that of the church are tested.

Chapter Two

The Issue of Faithfulness

In 1963 I was teaching in the Netherlands in the major seminary where I had previously studied myself. On March 21 our local bishop, Willem Bekkers, appeared on television on the Catholic broadcasting station. I knew the bishop well. He had been the parish priest of my home parish, and he had even been present at my first solemn Mass in my home town.

The television talks of Bishop Bekkers were very popular. The broadcasts could be seen all over the country and in Flemish-speaking Belgium. The topic for that night was birth control, and everyone was glued to their sets.

Robert Blair Kaiser, who served as *Time* magazine's Rome correspondent during the Council, calls that broadcast "the first open break in the dike" in the church discussion on the topic. It is a debate that has never stopped.

During the broadcast Bishop Bekkers made a remark that has remained with me ever since. He said, "There may be certain situations in which it is impossible to be mindful of all and every Christian and human value at the same time."[1]

In other words, faithfulness became an issue. There seemed no longer to be a ready-made, clear-cut answer for every moral problem we might encounter. Being faithful presented a different and more complicated challenge than we had supposed or been taught. The challenge we faced was remaining faithful in a time of shift and change from old to new. It was the challenge posed when a homogeneous society begins to move, the circle starts to widen, and the table starts to expand.

This is a practical difficulty I have experienced often in my life. When I was teaching at the University of Kenya I was frequently asked to serve on committees to screen job applicants. In many instances, these jobs were not academic ones. I sat in to decide on the hiring of sweepers and cleaners, maintenance people, cooks, and drivers. I was not asked because I was particularly versed in any of these tasks. I was asked to be there simply because I was a foreigner.

The other members of those committees belonged to the different ethnic Kenyan groups. They were blood relatives to the job applicants. If they did not pick their kinsperson— though he or she might be unqualified for the job—they would be accused at home of having betrayed their kin. At the same time, they had to consider the good of the university. If they hired an unsuitable person they would be accused by the university of acting irresponsibly. My function on the committee was to allow them to say at home—and to the university authorities—that I was responsible for the decision.

In a way it is not fair to give this Kenyan example to illustrate what I mean. It is a situation we all know from our own environment. It happens all over, all the time.

It is the problem of the soldier who serves his country, though he knows he is bound to a wider human community; it is the paradox of the salesperson and the manufacturer who have to serve the expectations of their shareholders while at the same time remembering their obligations to the community at large. Can we live without betrayal in our contemporary world? Can we remain faithful to all we believe in? Can we live without compromising ourselves economically, socially, ecologically, religiously? Can I be totally devoted to the interests of one nation in a world that is a global reality?

Asking those questions is not a pleasant task; often, it is an unwelcome task. Refusing to face them, however, does not solve anything. The church faces the same type of problem. It is a problem that goes back to the very beginning of Christianity, to the argument between James and Peter, and the difficulties between Peter and Paul. James, the brother of Jesus in Jerusalem wanted to restrict his circle to the family and acquaintances of Jesus. Peter did not agree; you had to cast your nets wider. Yet he, in turn, wanted to limit the church to Jewish Christians. Paul objected to that restriction. You had to be willing to welcome everyone. In Christ there was no Jew or Gentile. All had become one. Both James and Peter wanted to be faithful to something old, but had to give something up so as not to betray the new.

When Luke describes how the poor were helped, in the early Christian community—that first "global" community willing, in the name of Jesus, to embrace everyone—he reports that both Hebrew and gentile widows were supported. But he also reports how this ideal was betrayed. The Hebrew widows got the fat of the soup, and the widows of gentile stock got the thin. (Acts 6:1)

It remains a problem with the church.

Can I remain a denominational Christian welcoming only some to the communion table? How can I pray with the words of the psalms, in which I read terms like "them" and "us," and that are filled with a piety linked with enmity, even in the loveliest of them? Can I celebrate Jesus' intentions with a national flag above the altar? Paradoxes such as these confront the pope, as much as the rest of us.

These are challenges that arise in particular at moments of growth, at the moments when our circle opens itself to others.

Let me illustrate this with an example from Luke's Gospel. Luke describes how Jesus returns to his home town in Nazareth after his baptism by John, his forty days in the desert, and his first campaign of teaching and preaching throughout the countryside of Galilee. On the Sabbath day he goes to the local synagogue, as he has many times before. He volunteers to do the reading and they hand him the scroll of the prophet Isaiah. He opens the scroll and reads the passage which proclaims the coming of the new era, the era of the Lord's favor. His listeners are amazed and enthusiastic when he announces, "Today in your hearing this text has come true" (Lk 4:21). They look at one another. This is what they had been hoping for so long.

Yet the mood changes completely when Jesus goes on to imply that the Lord's favor would not only be for them in their village, Nazareth, nor even for their nation alone, but for the whole world. They feel betrayed. They even want to kill him. They jump up and hustle him to a cliff outside of town, intending to hurl him over the edge. This time he escapes.

Throughout his subsequent ministry, Jesus faces a similar reaction whenever he tries to open the circle of God's favor to those deemed "sinners," "outsiders," beyond the pale. It is this same opening of the circle that Jesus left as his dynamic legacy to the church. It is a dynamism that often continues to cause the same kind of problems in the very heart of the church itself. The church cannot but be faithful to that dynamism; and yet so often the church betrays it.

It is a scenario I know from my own pastoral experience. It is the sad story of the church in the Netherlands. During the Second Vatican Council, in dioceses all over the country, discussion groups were organized to read the Bible together, helping the members to discover their own dignity, their value, and their potential. In doing this, they discovered something their medieval co-patriot, the mystic Jan van Ruusbroec, had noted in his book, *The Spiritual Espousals*, some centuries before: "Now the grace of God flows from within us, and not from outside us, for God is more interior to us than we to ourselves."[2]

This was a discovery the church leadership did not appreciate, as it was almost directly at odds with their notion of authority as power coming from outside and imposed from above by ecclesial structures. The participants were encouraged to take themselves seriously as the People of God, and when they did this they found themselves in difficulties. They were helped to outgrow their constraints, they became more mature in their faith, they took up new responsibilities, and started asking for a greater role in decision making. But the church leadership did not grow with them. It is in such periods that faithfulness becomes difficult.

A British psychiatrist, Dr. Jack Dominian, describes the plight of many Christians today:

> For many people the moment they enter the church they feel diminished as persons, coupled with the vague notion that the minister is the important person who becomes the link between themselves and God. This combination of diminution, passivity, and helplessness is incompatible with the growing awareness of competence, skill, knowledge, and power that contemporary woman and man feels is her and his due.[3]

What to do in this situation where you are not breaking the bread, but the bread is broken for you? Not all church members could stand this new situation, not all were willing to accept and to live with the tension caused. Many simply gave up on the church. They opted out.

In Great Britain only 5-15% of the population attend church regularly. In the *Lutheran World Information* of December 1989 two recent polls in West Germany were cited. One showed that 80% of the population describe themselves as Lutherans or Catholics; the other showed that only 5% of Lutherans and 25% of Catholics regularly attend church services. According to a Gallup survey of 1988, 78 million Americans do not belong to a church or synagogue, a number that has risen from 61 million in 1978.

This does not mean, however, that the sense of God has disappeared. According to the same survey, about three-quarters of all Americans believe that Jesus is God and state that they pray to God. Fifty-four percent attend a church service each month.[4] Two-thirds believe that the Bible is "either the literal or the inspired word of God."

Clearly, however, there is a growing disaffection with church practices. Fifty-nine percent think that the churches spend too much time on organizational issues, such as how to raise more money, and 32% feel that organized religion is too restrictive.

Even in Great Britain, where the number of churchgoers is so low, 74% of the population believe in God and 69% believe that Jesus was the Son of God.[5]

This experience of God is not confined to statements made in surveys. Research conducted at Oxford shows that 48% of a random sample of the British population claim to have had a religious experience at least once in their lives.

One might also point to the world-wide concern for moral issues. Of course, there is no necessary link between morality and religiosity. Yet, morality concerns right and wrong, good and evil; one could say that in all moral issues there is reference to an absolute sense of value, a transcendent reality to be realized, a "Reign" to come. This is a sense of reality expressed not only in religion, worship, and morality, but also in music, painting, poetry, literature, and other kinds of artistic and scientific expression. Certainly, there is a great preoccupation with issues of personal morality: sex, alcohol, drugs, abortion, and so forth. But increasingly there is recognition of the moral dimension of social issues—issues of justice, peace, poverty, racism, homelessness, unemployment, the rights of women and children.

And so while many churches remain empty, people continue to be interested in God, morality, art, and one another, yearning for something that will bring us together in an attitude of respect and love, so that we can heal the world in which we live with a view to the new earth and new heaven to come.

The challenge of faith remains. Our faithfulness to that challenge is often the very reason many of us are no longer drawn to an institutionalized form of religion that does not sufficiently respect our sensitivities and needs. Such a church, characterized by bureaucracy, denominationalism, and provincialism, can seem all too much part of a world that troubles us.

Our Jesus community should be different.

Chapter Three

The Process of Healing

The sense that the world is sick is not new. The prophets of Israel as well as other religious traditions long ago expressed that feeling. The hope of healing is not new either. Western literature abounds with utopian stories and legends from Plato to Marx, not to mention the self-help books that abound in our shopping malls.

What we really need are not prophecies, utopias, or lists of advice. We need the actual healing process itself.

There is one author in our sacred scriptures who describes what happened around Jesus from that point of view. He did not develop a complicated theology. He did not look so deeply into the significance of symbols. He simply described groups of people who lived a new alternative to the usual human condition, and the hope that such communities offered. This was a hope he wanted to share. He resembles us more closely than any other New Testament writer.

His name is Luke. We do not know exactly where he came from. In fact, he hardly speaks directly about himself. He is most probably not a Jew. He is a gentile, or in other words, a pagan, though it is safe to assume that he was not a total stranger to the Jewish world.

In a way, he is representative of our own world. He is an outsider. He is not an apostle; he never met Jesus. Professionally, he is most probably a physician — or so tradition has supposed. There are, of course, scholars who question this tradition. But others observe that Luke employs at least four hundred medical-sounding words in his two books, his Gospel and the Acts of the Apostles. At the very least, he describes miracles, diseases, and symptoms with more clinical precision than is true with the other evangelists. Twice Luke has Jesus describing *himself* as a physician (Lk 4:23, 5:31). It is not unreasonable to believe that he is the one of whom Paul wrote, "Greetings from our dear friend, Luke, my doctor" (Col 4:14).

Whether or not he is a doctor, Luke is obviously good at diagnosing the world in which he lives. He is an intellectual struggling with the paradigms of his time. He thinks critically about what he sees. And there is obviously much to criticize.

In the very beginning of his gospel, an angel announces the birth of John the Baptizer to his father Zechariah. That angel expresses Luke's feelings. The angel speaks about a generation gap that has to be healed, about righteousness that has to be restored. According to Luke the world around him appears to be seriously sick. When he describes the first public appearance of Jesus in the synagogue of his hometown, Nazareth, the background of the story is a sick and corrupt world: sight has to be restored, oppression must be overcome, and prisoners liberated. His diagnosis is grave. Poverty and neglect are symptoms of serious structural problems: rulers have to be overthrown and structures changed. His prognosis must have been grim, as well. Otherwise Luke would not have been so surprised when he met the followers of Jesus.

But then something happens to him. He meets a Christian community. First one, but then others — a whole network that is new to him. We don't know where Luke met his first Christian community. It might have been in Troas, or maybe at Antioch. In any case, he finds a type of empowered life he has never seen before. He discovers in his sick world communities that are healing points, even in places like Corinth and Ephesus—in Luke's day, just about the most immoral places one could think of.

Luke is amazed by what he experiences. Like a typical intellectual, he records his reactions in two books. In those writings he describes not only his amazement about those communities, but also how surprised he is by the individuals he meets in them, and especially by the Spirit that seems to empower their lives. Repeatedly he reports how he hears them say, "It has seemed good to the Holy Spirit and to us . . ." (Acts 15:28). Over thirty times he remarks on that *immediate* divine direction.

He sums up his experience of the community when he notes how Jesus tells them before leaving, "But you will receive power when the Holy Spirit comes on you; and you will be my witnesses . . . to the ends of the earth" (Acts 1:8). In that text Luke records his own understanding of where the spirit of the community comes from. It is Jesus' Spirit.

> Luke has no doubt of the immediate explanation of these remarkable people he has met, of this fast-grow-ing, morally creative and redemptive community he has encountered. These are men and women "possessed," indwelt, and endued, by the living God, immanent in each as the Holy Spirit—or, as Luke says, very signifi-cantly, "the Spirit of Jesus" (Acts 16:7).[6]

It is not directly from Jesus that Luke discovers this. He does not meet Jesus. He never did. Rather, he detects the *risen life* of Jesus, the Spirit of Jesus, in the Christian com-munities he has met. It is in the communities that Luke encounters Jesus. And it is the same for the readers of Luke's Gospel.

Thus, Luke introduces his Gospel to the reader, Theo-philus: "I have decided to write an orderly narrative for you so as to give you *authentic* knowledge about the matters of which you have been informed" (Lk 1:3–4). Readers like

Theophilus had never met the Lord. They would only be able to find the Spirit of Jesus in the Christians they met. They would only meet him in the breaking of the bread of fellowship. Without that experience, the news about Jesus would just remain a splendid tale, a wishful dream, and anyone interested in the healing of the world would have to look elsewhere.

Luke describes all this in a beautiful way at the end of his Gospel in the story of the two disciples who are walking from Jerusalem to Emmaus.

Some have noted that Emmaus was not a village at all, as the text suggests, but a military camp of the Roman occupying forces, about seven miles from Jerusalem. This would add a particular edge to the story, especially if the two were working for the Roman troops. Their hope for a liberator of the Jewish people would appear especially poignant.

We might say that the two had taken an Easter holiday. We might conjecture that they went to Jerusalem because they had heard about Jesus' royal and slightly riotous reception as a king the week before. They must have taken that weekend off hoping that the Messiah would arrive, liberating Israel from its foreign yoke. But nothing of the kind had happened.

Now they are on their way back home and they meet Jesus, whom they do not recognize. He does not reveal his identity to them. He asks them why their faces are so long. They halt in their tracks, so eager are they to explain what has happened — or worse, what has not happened. They feel deceived. They tell the stranger how Jesus had been arrested, how he had been crucified, and also the strange report that he had risen from the dead.

Although they have heard the resurrection story, that is not their main interest. They are interested in something else. They are interested in changing the world. And, clearly, that has not happened. What does a resurrection from the dead mean when nothing else changes? Lazarus was raised; so what? The son of that widow at Nain was brought back to life, which was nice for his mother, and even — possibly! — for him; but what about the rest? There was even the story about another young girl, who had seemed to be dead, and who was awakened by Jesus. Again, so what? All those three would die again.

But at this point Jesus takes over. We don't know exactly what he tells them, but his teaching lasts the rest of the journey, until they arrive at their house. He agrees to stay with them. He sits down at their table and *breaks bread* with them. And immediately they recognize him. Whatever he was telling them, it must have had something to do with that breaking of the bread, or in other words, with a different *risen* or *healed* lifestyle. He must have been telling them that the Messiah would not merely bring a political delivery of the Jewish people as such. He would bring something much more incisive and decisive than that. He would introduce a new, alternative, healed lifestyle in which finally the whole of humanity would share their bread together.

At the moment that he breaks bread with them, they recognize him: It is he! The Messianic reign has begun! And at that same moment — as if he would not wish to hinder them in their own mission — Jesus disappears from their midst. But they are so taken by the new life revealed to them that they go all the way back to Jerusalem to tell the others.

This is the story of Luke himself. In the breaking of bread among the Christian communities he discovered and recognized the risen life of the Lord. It is a life attuned to the original intention of creation, a humanity sharing in God's gift of life, a community in which each person reaches out to the rest of the world in a *whole*-some, healing way.

And we, contemporary Christians, are in the same position as Luke. We are not going to meet Jesus personally; we meet him only through the communities formed in his memory.

That is how I first encountered Jesus. Though baptized a Christian within a few hours of my birth, I discovered what the risen life of Jesus was about in my experience with Christian communities.

It began with my family. It was in the context of my family and our parish that I started to think of becoming a missionary. Though in those days that call had more to do with assuring heavenly bliss to those we considered poor pagans than with the healing of this world, the latter aspect of our Christian faith was never completely overlooked.

Our community was engaged in the healing of this world. My father was, together with his friends, involved in all kinds of discussions about how to organize a socially just society. Their commitment went beyond mere words. In their deeds, as well, I discovered the power of the risen life of Jesus, which contradicted the evil powers at work in the world.

Somewhere in Israel there is a forest named after a Dutch hero in the resistance movement during the Nazi occupation of the Netherlands. The name of the forest is Joop Westerweel. In that forest there is a cedar tree with my name. The tree was offered to my father but he gave it to me. It was presented to him because he had helped some Jewish families to hide from the Nazis.

It would have been impossible to do such a thing on his own. He did it together with my mother and some other parishioners. It was a very dangerous venture. Discovery would have meant a horrible death for all involved. Being a child at the time, I never knew exactly what was going on, though in fact I played a small role. I only heard the full story afterwards.

The hidden families not only needed shelter, but food. This was a serious difficulty in a time when food was rationed and only available with coupons. Food was so scarce in those days that I would ride my bike to a farm more than ten miles out of town to buy *one* egg!

The hidden Jewish families needed ration cards. Friends of friends stole those coupons from a municipal office about twenty miles from my town. That is where I came in. I had to fetch those stolen coupons. I was not supposed to know what they were. They were given to me in a big yellow envelope which I had to pin to my undershirt. I was not supposed to stop along the way. I was not allowed to talk to anybody. And I had to avoid all police and other roadblocks.

My role was far from heroic, but later, when they wanted to offer a tree to my father, he asked that it be offered in my name. It represented my small part in an activity organized by a Christian community to heal one of the glaring wounds of the world at that time.

Years later I had another experience of Jesus' risen life at work in the community. I was a student in Rome. The headquarters of the Missionaries of Africa, where I lived, was located not far from the Vatican overlooking a valley called *Valle del'Inferno*. It was a sad place. Poor people who came mainly from the south of Italy and who had not yet found employment in Rome could not get any housing in town. There were anti-migration laws that prohibited them from being able to send their children to Roman schools. The most urgent need, however, was for housing. They lived in something like tents made out of paper and cardboard, or sometimes simply a hole in the ground, filled with some straw and covered with a blanket during the night.

They had to find shelter on land owned by others, which was illegal. But there was a loophole. If anyone managed to build a roof over his head without being discovered, he was safe. The owner could not simply destroy the dwelling.

A neighboring Christian community helped the poor to take advantage of this legal loophole. We would collect and hide building materials during the day. As soon as it became dark we would gather our materials and construct the mandatory roof, taking care to make as little noise as possible.

This activity had its daring aspects, since it was clearly against the law. If caught we would be in serious trouble. The landowners and the municipality were prepared to defend their rights—sometimes with violence. That is why we took care to post sentries to ward off curious onlookers, and even to bribe patrolling policemen with a bottle of wine.

That group was not the only presence around us in Rome of Jesus' risen life. Other communities took care of orphans and other people in need. But it was my most thrilling and in a way my most romantic encounter with Christ's spirit. Wherever I have traveled in the world, I have found that same *energy* at work.

As a teacher in the Netherlands I was in contact with a student community that assisted "guest laborers," as they were euphemistically called—most of them from North Africa and Turkey. They were in a foreign country, lost, unaware of their rights, and consequently often exploited. Local boarding houses would rent one and the same bed out four times a day. The workers, who could find no other lodging, slept in the same bed for shifts of six hours each and yet had to pay the price as if they had had the bed for twenty-four hours. That student community tried to assist these foreigners, getting others interested in their plight, and trying to organize on their behalf.

Later, when I was a professor and Catholic chaplain at the State University of Nairobi, our student parish became interested in the plight of the so-called "parking boys." These boys—and sometimes girls, too—had left their upcountry villages because their parents were incapable of buying the obligatory school uniforms or pay the school fees. Regulations have changed since then, but at that time primary schools were only free of charge for four years; after that, a fee was required. A large number of children—often the more intelligent ones—understood that there would be no future for them in their villages. Allured by the bright lights of the city, they ran away from home.

In Nairobi, the capital city of Kenya, they could take care of themselves rather well for the first six weeks or so. In fact they were often better off than at home. They found food in the dustbins and around the markets. They washed cars, made some money, and could go to the cinema and buy soft drinks.

The difficulties began when they had been in the city for some time, without sanitation, with a deficient diet, and suffering consequent illness. In their growing anguish, many started to use drugs. Having no money, they often resorted to the cheapest "high" available. They would hide at gas stations and wait until one of the customers had been served. When the station attendants were inside, they would run out, shake the remaining drops of gas from the nuzzle of the pump onto some rags, and start to inhale the fumes. They experienced a momentary intoxication, little realizing the damage they were inflicting on themselves.

I remember how we discussed all this, looking for some way to help. The difficulty was knowing how to approach the children, who fled away as quickly as birds from any contact with outsiders. Then one student had the idea of reaching them through music and dancing, which all African children love. She suggested that we use the social hall of the chaplaincy. So we opened the windows wide, found ourselves a band, and started to play at midday when some of those parking boys were usually roaming the neighborhood. It was a great success. In no time the parking boys came to dance, and our contact was made. The street kids explained that what they were really looking for was a school. And so an informal school was started, not only using the social hall but even the chapel itself.

From all over the city volunteers joined in the effort and a whole new program of charity was started called, appropriately, *Undugu*, brother/sisterhood. Another healing process had begun. Another wound had begun to heal.

Today in the United States I constantly come upon such efforts—groups lobbying for social justice, rehabilitation schemes, soup kitchens, peace groups, solidarity efforts, the sanctuary movement, ecology activists. Their variety itself is amazing.

The life of Christ, the life of the risen Lord, the life of a risen humanity bubbles up in all kinds of persons — Mother Teresa, Martin Luther King, Jr., Dorothy Day, to name only some of the best known in this country. Yet this is not something visible only in the special saints. There is a sufficient supply of this life for everyone.

It is a life that is noticeable every time someone breaks through the small circle of personal identity to reach out to the whole. No one can be healed — or to put it another way, no one can be "wholed," while remaining locked up in his or her own personal circle.

This is what Luke discovered in the Christian communities which he — a physician — diagnosed as "healed" and "healing." Luke traced that healing power to the spirit of the risen life of Jesus within them. It was Luke who formulated that phrase, "the Spirit of Jesus."

Once he had experienced that Spirit, once he had picked up their vision, he felt the need to announce that risen life to the whole of the wounded and suffering world.

It kept his heart, and the hearts of so many others, burning. And if we agree with Luke's original diagnosis of this world, and identify with his discovery of God's healing power, do not our hearts burn, too, with that same fire?

Chapter Four

People of God

Whenever you use the word *church* you immediately find yourself in difficulty. What exactly are you talking about? Church members, who should be aware that *they are church*, often do not think about themselves, when using the word, but of the pope, the bishops, and priests: in other words, the clerical hierarchy.

Yet the experiences I described in the preceding chapter rarely had anything directly to do with the church hierarchy. Rather, my personal experience of the risen life of Jesus happened in encounters with "ordinary" Christians in their communities, pursuing grassroots initiatives on a voluntary basis. These groups were like *churches within the Church.*

It must have been like this from the very beginning. It is in these types of grassroots communities that Luke meets the spirit of Jesus at work.

Reading his report you cannot escape the impression that Luke enjoys telling us how he met that spirit in persons and situations where the official leadership did not expect it. You can see that in his economy of words as an author. While the call of official church leaders like Peter, James, and John get seven verses, that of Zacchaeus gets ten. The story of the conversion of the chief treasurer of the Queen of Ethiopia takes up fourteen verses. The conversion of the outsider Paul is repeated three times, using forty-five verses in all. And finally there is the story of the calling of Cornelius on which Luke spends no less than sixty-six verses!

Like the story of the travellers to Emmaus, once again these stories are really Luke's story. He clearly relishes telling how Peter had to be persuaded to accept the gentile Cornelius in Joppa. Luke must have enjoyed being able to add that Cornelius had his own visions — very much like Peter's — and how Peter was surprised to see that Cornelius and his family received the gift of the Holy Spirit.

Twice Peter has to admit in these reports that they "received the Holy Spirit just as we did. . . . God gave them no less a gift than he gave us when we came to believe in the Lord Jesus Christ. How could I stand in their way?" (Acts 10:47; 11:17)

When a storyteller repeats a story like that twice in great detail, you can be sure he wants to make something clearly understood! Luke wants to emphasize that the whole of humanity is in the same situation. He best explains what was happening when he coins the phrase, "the Spirit of Jesus" (Acts 16:7). The implication of that expression is that we all have access to the same experience, the same wholeness and holiness, the same understanding, and the same mystery.

The issue is not new.

In the preface to his famous translation of the New Testament (1516), the great Erasmus wrote:

Maybe it is right to veil the secrets of kings, but the mystery of Christ must be revealed publicly. I wish women to be able to read the gospels and Paul's epistles; I want the weaver to be able to sing them as he works, the traveller to make them into companions along the weary way. Baptism, the sacraments, are common to all Christians. Why then should the principles of doctrine remain the prerogatives of those we call theologians and monks and who are only a very limited part of the Christian people? . . . All those inspired and lifted up by the Spirit of Christ possess the true theology, be they grave-diggers or weavers.

The church is not divided into simple ones who have to listen, and others who know more and who are initiated in a special way into the mystery. To continue to believe that would be to yield to a deadening gnosticism. It would be a serious obstacle to any healthy growth of the community — especially in our time, so often called the age of information. To act as if the Spirit, faith, and knowledge, are by divine dictate reserved only to some becomes increasingly unacceptable.

Yet it is a belief that is still widespread and carries serious consequences for the way believers judge themselves.

Let us offer an example.

I am thinking of a nurse in a large hospital in this country, well trained and highly efficient. She does a good job, is kind and pleasant to her patients. Yet she is dissatisfied with her way of life. After praying and attending some retreats she comes to the conclusion that she would really like to do something directly for the Reign of God here on earth.

She contacts a mission organization that is willing to send her out as an associate. She follows the training program and goes overseas to work in a hospital. She remains there for three years. That is the limit allowed by the organization that sent her out. She is now back in the same hospital from which she left.

The strange thing about her story is that in her mind and that of the church she only seemed to be working for the growth of the Reign of God while "volunteering." It was only in the context of a religious, clerical set-up that she was able to integrate her profession in view of the Reign of God. Once back in her original parish community, things are again as they were before she left.

Another example.

A married man with a family works professionally in a church context overseas for a number of years. He does a marvelous job as a development organizer. But at a certain point he feels he should return home for the education and "rooting" of his children. He would have liked to do similar work in his home country. But back home he cannot be professionally engaged in church work. He is still looking for a job in a church context, which he would prefer to the "secular" business world, which he finds materialistic and corrupt.

His family and friends tell him that he shouldn't be so judgmental. They say he is practically condemning the whole world in such a way. But he is not convinced. He believes that only in a church—by which he means a more or less clerical—context can he work with integrity.

Both cases point to serious weaknesses in our Christian approach. The "Spirit of Jesus" might be with us, except when it comes to our daily professional life. In the case of the nurse, she was not helped in her own community to see the relation between her work and the healing ministry that is what the Christian community is all about. Likewise, the development worker did not see that his professional work, despite the fact that it was done outside an institutional clerical church context could be a healing one.

The Spirit of Jesus reaches into our hearts and minds, but too seldom does it enter into our daily activities. All too often, when lay people talk about joining in the work of the church, they are thinking about sharing clerical jobs in their free time. Their own daily work doesn't seem to qualify!

A doctor volunteers some hours in a roadside clinic. A lawyer spends some of his free time offering legal advice to people unable to pay a consultancy fee. A builder helps construct a church barn on his weekend. A teacher helps out in the Sunday school. It is as if there are two different worlds that meet in this way.

There is a dualism in the way lay people, clergy, and religious speak about the world, the church, themselves, and each other.

It is difficult to put your finger exactly at the point where this dualism begins. It was unknown in the first two centuries of the church. "Throughout the whole of the second century the main concern of Christians was to define themselves in relation to Christ rather than their role vis-à-vis each other."[7]

In the early centuries of the church, according to research done by the liturgist J.A. Jungmann, the Christian people as a whole, even during liturgical celebrations, were described as one people. In those days speaking about the church did not suggest the ambiguities we now find. *Church* was a word with one, univocal meaning. It meant the Christian community, the people of God. Further distinctions were neither felt nor intended. Up to the end of the second century the term *iereus* (priest) was used exclusively to describe Christ and, subsequently, the Christian people as a whole, without it being used to indicate those who preside over the celebration.[8] It was only later—especially after the Edict of Milan in 313—that the whole position of the church in the world began to change. Gradually, clergy and laity began to look at each other and their role division, rather than at a world that has to be healed. It is at that time that the church became an official institution, with all the usual bureaucratic trappings and temptations.

During the centuries that followed a clericalization of the liturgy and, subsequently, of spirituality, occurred. Clergy and laity began to speak a different language. Christians no longer met in houses or market halls as they did before. Special buildings were constructed as churches with the nave, occupied by the lay people, clearly differentiated from the sanctuary and the choir.

Unleavened (i.e., "special," not ordinary) bread was used for the Eucharist. It was distributed by a standing clergy to a kneeling laity, who were fed like infants with a little morsel of bread, placed directly on their tongues.

The Gregorian reforms of the XIth century mark an important step in this phenomenon of clericalization which now extends to spirituality. According to the spirituality of the time, lay people live in the midst of the secular world not because it is there that they find their specific vocation but because the status of the lay person is a concession to human weakness. From there it is but one step to claim that lay people have no part in the sacred order. ... In the end, the lay person is seen as nothing more than an eternal minor, living in the midst of the temptations of sin, *infants*, from the intellectual, spiritual, and liturgical point of view.[9]

Many prophetic voices have been raised against this clerical domination of the church. It would be impossible to review them all. One could cite St. Francis of Assisi, who refused ordination and who became the spokesperson for the lay movements of his time. More recently there was John Henry Newman, named a cardinal in his old age, but who wrote a famous essay in 1859 entitled, "On Consulting the Faithful in Matters of Doctrine."

A recent attempt to give the lay faithful their rightful place was during the Second Vatican Council. In the document on the church, the Council speaks of the whole church as one "People of God." This was a direct reaction against the tendency to identify the church with the clerical hierarchy.[10] The People of God, as a name for the church, refers to all those called together to be healed and, in turn, to heal. That healing is not something that happens in merely a clerical or sacramental fashion. It happens in concrete, mundane, and practical ways. Christians are no longer passive objects; they are active agents.

What Luke describes as the healing work of the communities he met was not only the work of a kind of clergy. It was the activity of a community composed of different professionals, united in heart and soul, *moving together with the Holy Spirit*, who were changing the world around them into a better place (Acts 4:31). That is why Luke speaks about

"the events that have taken place among us" in this world
(Lk 1:1). As one contemporary author said of them: "They
are good people to know."[11]

The nurse and the development worker, mentioned above,
would have no difficulty, I am sure, joining a community like
this and using their professional skills directly, together with
the other community members, in healing the materialistic,
sick, and disintegrating world around them.

This is the kind of church we need—made up of communities that take up the challenge that is raised by the defini-
tion of the church as "People of God."

It would be impossible to review all the developments in
this regard. But special mention should be made of the emer-
gence of the small groups called Basic Ecclesial Communities
that have sprung up in Latin America and other parts of the
world. Based on their consciousness of themselves as People
of God, these groups make the liturgy and preparation for
the sacraments their own. Their Christian faith concerns the
entirety of their daily lives. For them there is no hesitation
about the need for a sanctification of this world. Most of the
members of these communities are poor, cultivating the Spirit
of Jesus that moves them. They organize not only liturgical
units, but social, economic, and political self-help communities.

The growth of these communities has an important theological significance, not only for the poor, but for all of us,
including the rich and the middle classes, as the Brazilian
theologian Fr. Marcello Azevedo, S.J. notes: "The great challenge is how to carry the fundamental spirit of the Basic
Ecclesial Communities to other social milieus in the
church."[12]

This development did not occur only in Latin America; in
parts of Asia and in Africa, as well, the "People of God"
renewal prompted by Vatican II has stimulated the growth
of small Christian communities.

As Bishop Patrick Kalilombe, from the East African country of Malawi, has testified,

In the circumstances of East Africa, it is impossible to consider the missions or the parishes as the basic units of the local church. If we do so, the church will be doomed to failure. We must adopt a new system in which the basic unit of the church will be these smaller communities in which the ordinary life of the people takes place.[13]

I myself have experienced the life of those small Christian communities. Often they begin as prayer groups, reflecting on the Bible in the context of their daily lives. But they do not only pray; nor do they only reflect. They apply their response to the life of Jesus in their daily lives. The nurse begins to realize that her professional nursing itself should be seen as a direct continuation of the work of Jesus, through his Spirit alive in her. So does the policeman, the farmer, the teacher, the housekeeper, and everyone else.

This encounter with Jesus in the Bible leads them to a more human and divine organization of their community. They begin social support systems for the neglected and the marginalized, the sick and the poor. They put their gifts and talents, and often also their food and goods together. Their devotion and their zeal, their inculturated Christian contact with God in prayer, song, and dance—indeed, their joy— begins to attract others.

The community grows until they can no longer meet in one house. It is then that the group knows they are getting too large. So they split into smaller groups, which in turn begin to grow.

The late Cardinal Malula of Kinshasa in Zaire, a great African church leader, got into difficulties with the Roman authorities when the boundaries between the clergy and the laity began to blur. He responded unambiguously:

In the Church we need lay people who are not clericalized, who remain lay people while taking up their

responsibilities for evangelization and the organization
of the community. What pushed us . . . was our faith in
the sacraments of baptism and confirmation . . . in the
baptismal grace of the laity. [14]

This does not mean that those communities have no difficulties. Naturally they do. But so also did the communities
that Luke met. He gives some striking examples of their difficulties, their discriminations, their insincerities, jealousies,
and straightforward pettiness. Luke sees these problems as
unavoidable consequences of a process — the recovery process
of the human community.

Some studies of what has been happening in the basic
communities since Vatican II sound optimistic about these
developments. They even mention cautiously the disappear-
ance of the division between the laity and the clergy:

The Basic Ecclesial Communities are the cornerstones
of an integral ecclesiology. The division between laity
and priests no longer has any decisive significance,
whereas solidarity has become the principal issue. The
BECs have come to represent a form of particular
church whose dynamism is directed toward the future.
If the poor in Latin America, the blacks in South Africa,
the workers in rural areas in the Philippines are in process of discovering that their emancipation is not merely
a marginal issue for those who profess to be Christians,
then a new ecclesial awareness becomes possible. Inso-
far as they are in the process of making the Church their
own, a major step towards the integration of the laity
into an ecclesial community has been taken.[15]

There is good reason for caution. Not everyone in the hierarchy is enthusiastic about such developments.

In the 1970s the Catholic Episcopal Conference of Kenya
authorized the start of a development and education program

for existing small Christian communities. Its official title was Christian Development and Education Service (CDES). The service used the method of Paolo Freire's *Pedagogy of the Oppressed*. It developed programs and techniques that assisted people in their Christian communities to be themselves, to be aware of what was going on around them, and to become self-reliant.[16] It was at that very moment, when the programs were becoming successful and the people were really coming into their own, that difficulties began, not only with the government, but also with the ecclesial authorities. While the leaders of the communities began to come in for harassment from the government, the bishops at first closed CDES down and then reorganized it in a more centralized and hierarchical way.

The church hierarchy is often good at emancipation, but not so good at dealing with the emancipated. A proof of this might be seen in events in other parts of the world, where local churches responded in a different way to that new description of the church as "People of God."

In many countries steps were taken immediately after Vatican II to integrate lay faithful into the structures of the local church in parish councils or synods with lay participation. In some cases diocesan elections were held to fill these posts and for a while it looked as if lay people were really going to become active partners in shaping the direction of the church. But this euphoria didn't last. The "synodal" movement of the 1970s lost its momentum, in large part due to resistance from Rome and the bishops. In the final document of the Synod of Bishops held in 1985 to assess the results of Vatican II twenty years after the close of the Council, the term People of God was not even mentioned.

It is true that in the Council this term was complemented by other images of the church, such as Mystical Body of Christ; but failure even to mention the term could hardly be reconciled with the spirit of the Council. People of God, after all, was the Council's most esteemed image of the church.

The term did not utterly disappear. The next Synod in 1987 had as its theme the "Vocation and Mission of the Laity in the Church and the World Twenty Years after the Second Vatican Council." A document issued by the Synod was entitled "Message to the People of God."

Two years later, Pope John Paul II finally released a document on the Synod of 1987. It was entitled "The Lay Members of Christ's Faithful People."[17] In this long, laborious exhortation John Paul II states that "in its turn, the Council has looked again at the entire history of salvation and has reproposed the image of the church as the people of God. . . . " This passing reference hardly indicates the significance of this image of the church. In fact, the main point of the document is to show that the church is an institute divided between ordained clerics and nonordained lay people. They both have their own world to live in. The lay faithful's world is the secular one, though through baptism and confirmation they participate and share in the life of the clerical church.

> The ordained ministries, apart from the persons who receive them, are a grace to the entire church. These ministries express and realize a participation in the priesthood of Jesus Christ that is different, not simply in degree but in essence, from the participation given to all the lay faithful through baptism and confirmation. (n.22)

In a chapter entitled "Women and Men" the exhortation goes on to explain,

> Though not called to the apostolate of the twelve and thereby to the ministerial priesthood, many women nevertheless accompanied Jesus in his ministry and assisted the group of apostles (cf. Lk 8:2–3), were present at the foot of the cross (cf. Lk 23:49), assisted at the burial of Jesus (cf. Lk 23:55), received and transmitted the mes-

sage of the resurrection on Easter morn (cf. Lk 24:1–10) and prayed with the apostles in the Cenacle awaiting Pentecost. (cf. Acts 1:14). (n.49)

All of this is true. But why stop there? Why conclude that these various forms of accompaniment were all that the women did and were supposed to do? Why stop at the point when they are awaiting their empowerment at Pentecost?

It is again and again the temptation of the church to stop at Christmas, at Jesus' childhood, at his transfiguration, at the last supper, at the cross, at the resurrection, at the apparitions, at the ascension, or even as here at Pentecost. Yet it is only at that moment that life really began for them!

Luke was struck by the life that began among the disciples at that moment. He was struck not because he met a group of people who were trying to define their roles (though they did that too from time to time), but because they were all hit by the same spirit, the Spirit of Jesus.

Inspired by that Spirit, the healing and development of the world became their first order of business. The Spirit pervaded not only their hearts and minds, but their daily life and work.

It is not that all this is lost in John Paul II's exhortation. Yet, a chance seems to have been missed. I wonder who will be helped by such an exhortation. Even the term "exhortation" seems to smack of condescension.

According to those who were present in the Synod itself, John Paul II did not fully take their viewpoints into consideration. For example, themes that had been brought up by the African and Asian churches were entirely overlooked.

One of the issues brought up by those churches was inculturation. Inculturation has to do with the interaction between Christian faith and the local culture. This is a problem of vital interest to those churches where Westernized Christianity attempts to take root in non-Western cultures. But inculturation is not only a concern of non-Western churches.

When Cardinal Eduardo Pironio, head of the Pontifical Council for the Laity addressed thirty-five bishops and twenty-five Vatican officials some months after the publication of the exhortation in March 1989, he said,

> The lay faithful share fully in the common dignity of all God's children in the common call to holiness and in the evangelizing mission common to the whole church. However, it is not a sharing of a purely sociological and democratic type, but a sharing sacramentally established on the apostolic and Petrine ministry. The experience of living in a democratic society where citizens assume responsibility for the life of their local community, in the world of business, in educational and cultural institutions, etc., can lead to adopting in the church a sociological model of a human-historical democracy.[18]

Here is the inculturation of the church—not in African but in North American terms—that has the Cardinal worried. Democracy and equality, individual freedom and responsibility are the very air Western Christians breathe. How can they happily relate to the paternalistic way in which the Eucharist is conducted and the church run?

How can we fail to be shocked at the male domination that seems to be continued in the name of Jesus? In the diocese of Baltimore girls are allowed to "serve" at Mass. This is a great step forward toward normalization of relationships within the church. But a girl may not serve the way a boy does. A boy hands the water and wine cruets directly to the priest. A girl is not allowed to do that. She has to put the cruets on the altar, take a step backward, and then allow the priest to pick them up from there.

Can we expect youth, socialized in this way, to develop a clerical "vocation"? Can Christ not be better inculturated in the way we in the West relate to one another?

The Pope's exhortation is full of wariness and obvious fear

of loosing authority over a laity who want to be respected and treated as co-equal partners in the enormous task Jesus engaged us in. Such a laity is not perfect. But it is a laity that is self-aware, searching, well-informed, and world-conscious.

It is made up of the sort of person Luke addresses in his gospel, when he dedicates his books to someone he calls "His Excellency Theophilus." We don't know whether Theophilus was a real person or only a pseudonym. The term "excellency" could mean "best friend," or something like that. Luke uses the term three times in the Acts of the Apostles. In all those cases it is used to address formally a Roman official. From this some exegetes have drawn the conclusion that Luke was addressing some aristocratic Roman of the class which he probably once treated as a physician.

Thus, Luke addresses a class of emancipated, individualistic, affluent persons, freed from the preoccupation with survival, and consequently with time on their hands to ponder their further personal potential: persons whom many of us resemble.

It is to them—and to us—that Luke puts the case for Christianity.

Chapter Five

Modern Personality and the Spirit of Jesus

In all of the gospels there is only one story about Jesus' childhood. Luke describes Jesus' personal independence when, at the age of twelve, he makes it clear to his parents that his first commitment is not to them but to his mission and to his heavenly Father. Aside from the independence from his parents, there is another revealing element in the story: they find him in the temple, asking questions of the elder teachers.

Later in life Jesus displays the same personality and independence. There can be no doubt about his social and personal emancipation. There is something extremely modern about Jesus, in the degree to which he was submerged neither in his family network, his ethnicity, nor, unquestioningly, in his religion. This stance brought him on several occasions into deep conflict with his family and the religious authorities of his time. It is especially in his conflict with the Pharisees that we can learn more about his position.

Many Christians are accustomed to thinking of the Pharisees as the archenemies of Jesus. This is an oversimplification of the matter. Recent work in Jewish-Christian dialogue has provided us with an ever-growing insight into that fascinating Jewish movement for renewal. Some have even concluded that Jesus himself was "a Pharisee who engaged in intense interaction with other Pharisees."[19]

In a way the Pharisees were facing problems similar to the one we met in the preceding chapter. They were upset about the clericalization of the religious life of their people. Everything seemed to turn around the temple, while, in their view, worship of Yahweh should be expressed in faithfulness to the law and its works of justice and mercy in everyday life.

They did not want to abolish the temple service. They regretted the destruction of the temple at the time of the Babylonian exile. But they were not at all comfortable when, after the exile, the temple was rebuilt and reestablished as the dominant and principal center of worship. They relied in their anxiety on prophets like Amos, who had expressed Yahweh's indignation so forcefully:

> I take no pleasure in your sacred ceremonies.
> When you bring me your whole offerings
>   and your grain offerings
> I shall not accept them
> nor pay heed to your shared offerings of stall-fed
>   beasts.
> Spare me the sound of your songs;
> I shall not listen to the strumming of your lutes.
> Instead let justice flow on like a river
>   and righteousness like a never-failing current.
>   (5:21b–24)

In the eyes of the Pharisees, overemphasis on the temple cult stood in the way of realizing the meaning of true faithfulness. Yet the temple had not helped the people before the Babylonian exile and it was not helping them now. The Jews were again under foreign occupation—this time by the Romans. While the Pharisees opposed the Roman occupation, they realized that an armed revolution would be of no help. The real change needed was a spiritual renewal among the Jewish people. They wanted to liberate the people not just from the Romans but from the grip of the priests and the priestly party of the Sadducees.

They had gradually worked out a whole program of declericalization to realize their aim. Interestingly enough, this program seems to resemble quite a few of the aspirations of some church reformers of our own day:

1) They argued that the Sinaitic law was given by Moses to the whole people, to every individual, and not just to the priestly leaders. The traditional 613 commandments of the Hebrew Bible had to be carefully restudied to see how they could be implemented in concrete everyday life.

2) They gradually developed a new kind of religious lay leadership, the teacher or *rabbi*. The rabbi was no priest. His task was to interpret the law and to apply it to concrete situations of every day. The rabbis were not just academic scholars, reading books while sitting in their studies. They had to combine their teaching with concrete acts of mercy and healing. This was the ultimate test of their wisdom and their teaching.

3) The Pharisees developed the institution of the *synagogue*. It was not a replica of the temple. It was not so much the "house of God," but the "house of the People of God."[20] The synagogue was the communal focus. It was where courts of law were held, strangers were welcomed, alms were given, and questions were discussed.

4) In their efforts to reach the whole of the people in their daily lives, the Pharisees applied the commandment of the Law—"You will be to me a Kingdom of priests, my holy nation" (Ex 19:6)—to everyone. They reasoned that the temple altar in Jerusalem could be replicated at every table in the household of Israel and that everyone must keep the priestly laws.

Thus, Phariseeism changed the relation between God and humanity. God was related to each individual person. God was not only the Father of the Patriarchs or of the people of Israel as such. Each and every person had the inborn dignity, possibility, and right to address God directly as Father. God cared about *you*, was concerned about *you*, loved *you*. This personal love of God for each person was such that the Pharisees also believed in the resurrection of each person after their death. God loved *you* so much that God wished your unique self to live forever.

Considering all this, we might wonder why Jesus came into conflict with the Pharisees. Different explanations have been given. We know that the Pharisees were themselves divided into many schools of thought, of which the School of Shammai and the School of Hillel were the most important. Hillel upheld the possibility of salvation for the gentiles, a view which Shammai opposed. Jesus shared the view of Hillel, a source of conflict in itself, since in his time Shammai's school held sway.

But Jesus got all the Pharisees against him in his interpretation of our personal relation to God, and consequently our relation to the divine law. While the Pharisees acknowledged God as their communal and personal Father, Jesus called God "Abba," indicating a different degree of intimacy than the Pharisees were willing to accept. This new intimacy with God corresponded, of course, to a fresh understanding and experience of one's own personal dignity. That dignity prevails over everything else. At this point the Pharisees hesitated.

> The Pharisees gradually began to look upon Jesus' independent stress on the worth of the individual as a potential threat to Jewish communal survival. They were concerned with the absorption of Judaism by Hellenism and thus insisted on erecting what they termed "a fence around the Sabbath" as a safeguard against the destruction of the people of Israel.[21]

In a miracle like the liberation of a bent woman on the Sabbath day (Lk 13:10–17), the healing itself is not the issue.

The main problem is Jesus' deliberate assertion of the primacy of each woman and man as a person. As John Pawlikowski remarks, "Thus, while the Pharisees pushed the concept of each individual's worth a tremendous distance, Jesus stretched it to its final limits." The issue is, how far can one stress that primacy of the person without undoing the community? How do individual and society relate to each other in that case?

There was another complication. In Jesus' view God related to all human beings in this way without any exception. Jesus made this obvious in his words and deeds. For this reason, contrary to the conviction of the Pharisees, Jesus maintained that we should love and respect not only our friends but even our enemies. He continuously reached out in his healing and comfort to the poor of the land, the *am ha aretz*, who were looked down upon by the Pharisees, as so many gospel stories record (eg. Lk 18:9).

And there is yet another point, the issue of forgiveness, where the Pharisees attacked Jesus openly. Jesus was so conscious of his special and personal relationship with "Abba" that he claimed this power of forgiveness—which, according to the Pharisees, belonged exclusively to God—as his own, transferring it even to his followers. According to Jesus, our intimacy with God is so great that we share the power to reconcile. Jesus loved with God's love, and we should love in the same way.

The Pharisees were unwilling to go this far. In the eyes of many of them Jesus had become a real danger for their society. They could not see how you could teach and practice the human individualized personality of Jesus without endangering the communal identity of the Jewish people.

They continuously tried to catch Jesus and silence him. When they did not succeed in this, they began to threaten him. They tell him to leave the place because—they say—his life is in danger, Herod wants to kill him (Lk 13:31). John tells us how they finally came together to organize his execution. They give their reasons: "If we let him go on like this, everyone will believe in him, and our nation will be destroyed" (Jn 11:47–50).

They were scared. They were terrified in a way leaders often are. Think of bishops and theologians who agreed with what was decided during the Second Vatican Council on the role of the laity and who later got scared of their own initiatives and decisions when the laity went on to draw the logical conclusions.

The Pharisees had taken the initiative to liberate their people. That is why they started the rabbinate and the synagogue. But in Jesus they met a person—perhaps he was even one of them—who drew out all the implications of this emancipation program. What would happen should he succeed in empowering his followers in the same way? How would you be able to hold together a community or society composed of that type of individual?

It is not difficult to empathize with their feelings. Though in our own society no one is as self-possessed as Jesus, many of us seem to have come a long way—such a long way, indeed, that we are facing the issues those Pharisees in their council meeting long ago were afraid of. In fact, those problems are much more serious than they could have foreseen.

The question of how the new independent, self-possessed individual relates to society concerns not only interpersonal relationships, but issues of peace, justice, and the integrity of our environment. Our growing individuality, increased self-awareness, expanded self-possession and subjectivity, often turn the rest of reality into a mere object. We have difficulties relating to others and to our whole environment.

Increasingly free from the preoccupation with physical survival, we are within grasp of subduing the earth and controlling life. It is as if many of us remain locked up in our personal castles, considering total independence as our ideal. But this means defending ourselves against any possible infringement of our freedom, which in turn means trying to control everyone and everything around us.

Some years ago I participated in a meeting of philosophers from all over the world. Some of the participants were from the Soviet Union — in a time before the thaw of glasnost. One of them was amazed about his American contacts. When he wanted to sum up his impression of the West, he said: "You are so aware of yourselves, you have made yourselves into God."

We are no gods. Yet there is definitely some truth in this remark. Our own literature is very much aware of this development, and recent studies like Robert Bellah's *Habits of the Heart: Individualism and Commitment in America Life* (1985), Christopher Lasch's *The Culture of Narcissism* (1978), and an older study like David Riesman's *The Lonely Crowd* (1950), express their concern about this development. As long as one is embedded in a social structure, bound by an ethnic group, subject to social control, and afraid of sanctions, the issue of freedom does not easily arise. It is only at the moment when one has access to the principle of the *self* — apart from the others — that one can dispose of the self. It is only when one is *available* to self, that one can be *available* to others.

What happens then? What happens when you are in affirmative possession of self? What does a society look like when the majority are in that position? How do you organize its structures and support systems?

The actual church structures do not seem equipped to be of great help in this crisis. A mere statement that the church is no democracy, and that some have access to the Spirit in ways that others don't is of little help. Indeed, it only aggravates the crisis.

Dr. Jack Dominian poses the problem this way:

> The whole gospel was directed at the poor and our Lord himself enjoyed no riches. Indeed, the church is extremely well orientated when it comes to serving the poor. But what about those whose material needs are

being met? Have we reached a stage when thirty to forty percent of the world has to be spiritually disenfranchised? There is little evidence that the church has a plan for the affluent West except that it should use its riches to serve the poor. This is a policy of despair.[22]

It is not only a policy of despair but of consternation.

As we noted before, the crisis is not a new one. It is as old as the first emancipation process in humanity's sacred history. Take the case of Moses. He had difficulties in convincing his people to trust in God and in themselves, and to take their fate into their own hands. But as long as he was helping his people seek emancipation, he did not have the difficulties he encountered when that same people began to come into their own. They needed forty years in the desert to overcome that crisis and to get sufficiently organized to be able to move on. Emancipation has its price!

No wonder that the Pharisees—and together with them the Sadducees, the priests, the lawyers and scribes—were worried to see this liberated person Jesus walking through their streets, propagating his ideals, conscientizing people all around him. He had to be stopped. Didn't he understand the difficulties he was causing?

There is at least one instance in the gospel where they decided to confront him directly with their question. In the gospel of Matthew it is the Pharisees who ask the question, while in Luke it is a lawyer who addresses him:

"Rabbi, which is the greatest commandment in the law?" The question is more complex than it may at first appear. Behind it lie these questions: When you stress the dignity of the individual person as much as Jesus does, how are you going to organize society? How do God, the self, and community relate to each other? How do you prioritize? Which is the most important law?

He answered, "Love the Lord your God with all your heart, with all your soul, and with all your mind. That

is the greatest, the first commandment. The second is
like it: Love your neighbor as yourself. Everything in the
law and the prophets hangs on these two commandments." (Mt 22: 31–41)

In Matthew Jesus gives the answer. In Luke's gospel he
does not. Remaining in character, he asks his interrogator to
answer the question himself. After all, the question is about
how to handle one's own emancipation. The answer is the
same: "You must love the Lord your God with all your heart,
with all your soul, with all your strength, and with all your
mind, and your neighbor as yourself" (Lk 10:27). Jesus
answers: "You are right, do this and life is yours!"

Jesus answers these questions as directly as they have been
asked. And his answer addresses all the worries of his ques-
tioners. How can you be the emancipated personality Jesus
propagated in his lifestyle and word, and yet relate to community and the transcendent? What would a spirituality look
like when developed for those affluent and independent
enough to afford the luxury of individualism?

The problem is not just one for the Pharisees of Jesus'
time. It is also a real question for the 30-40% of the world's
mostly Western, mostly Christian affluent population.

Jesus' answer is short and simple. It is an old answer, too.
Three factors have to be taken into consideration: self, the
other, and God. Two directives have to be taken into account
when relating, combining, and prioritizing our relations to
those three. There is one functional energy involved: love.
Three reduced to two; and two seen as one.

Chapter Six

Loving the True

A few years ago a little booklet appeared called "Our Best Kept Secret." It was about the social teachings of the church. It is true that the social teachings of the church are not well known. However, this is not really the best kept secret. There is another "secret" that remains hidden. It is very simple: God loves us. God loves each of us with the same divine, all-encompassing and merciful love.

This is the mystery "hidden from the foundation of the world" and revealed in the life of Jesus. It is the message of his life, reaching out to everyone with the same love, even to those marginalized by their own society. It is that love that lies at the basis of his "social teaching."

Every time Jesus lifted the veil of this mystery he got into serious trouble. When he told his own townsfolk in Nazareth that the goodness and joy he brought in the name of God were not only for them, but for everyone, they got so terribly upset that they reacted with a riot against him.

It is the same mystery Jesus disclosed in a story like the one about the prodigal son — a mystery that was truly scandalous to the prodigal's older brother. He could not believe his ears when they told him how his father received his younger brother. This can't be true, he thought. But it was true. It is true — and not only for you and me, but for those we consider our greatest enemies. God created us, all of us, because God delights in life, and wants to share this utter delight.

In our days this can sound utterly banal and sentimental. I have related my niece's reaction when I gave her a sticker that read "God loves you." "What a bore!" she sighed. The word love has been so overused and trivialized that it doesn't mean anything anymore. It might be that the Pharisees reacted in the same way when Jesus answered their question about how to organize an individualized and personalized society with the words *love* and *God*.

Yet, I wonder whether there was not more to their reaction. Matthew reports that after Jesus' answer, none of them dared to ask him any more questions. Were they afraid that too much of the mystery of God's love for everyone would be revealed?

Sometimes I wonder whether the impasse in all this is not something—consciously or maybe unconsciously—intended by those in power. Do they want the truth to be revealed? One of the prime mechanisms of power is the idea that God loves some persons better than others. Perhaps this would account for the reaction of some of Jesus' powerful enemies. They were confronted in Jesus with the power of God's love, spilled out, broken, and shared with the multitude, the rabble, with sinners.

What lover of control likes to be reminded that his or her access to the power line is not something exceptional, unique, but given to all? If the foundation of our human existence is that God loves us all in the same way, then we all have the same access to that power.

The story is told of a young priest who was captivated by this idea and who preached it in the presence of his much older and more experienced pastor, who suddenly awoke from a peaceful slumber to hear his young colleague stressing that God loved the parishioners in exactly the same way as God loved the pastor and himself. To strengthen his argument he added that this was the reason Jesus forbade anyone to call another human being *father*, *teacher*, or *master*. Once the service was over and the two met in the privacy of the sacristy, the older priest told the younger one never to preach in that way again. He added: *"Not because it is not true, but because it would be the end of us!"*

So it would. But more than that. Accepting this truth would upset the whole existing ecclesial and societal order. It is a truth that invalidates the way our society is organized from top to bottom. It upsets practically all existing relationships. It makes the life we are living at the moment a *lie*.

Apartheid and racism are based on the denial of that truth, but so also are the economic inequalities and the social class structures that are integral parts of our social system.

Really believing that God loves the other as much as God loves us would make it impossible for us to tolerate homeless people freezing in the streets, starving babies dying in Ethiopia, and the use of our money for manufacturing poisonous gas, nuclear arms, and suchlike things.

In the eyes of many, there are really very valid reasons for hiding this truth at all costs. The denial of this truth lies at the bottom of all kinds of slavery and oppression, old and new. Within the context of the church it must have been one of the reasons that the reading of the Bible was forbidden to the "common folk" for so long in our own regions, and that translations in the vernacular were frowned upon not only long ago in the West, but even as recently as the 1930s in Africa.

But this kind of maneuver is not simply a matter of the distant past. It happens still in all kinds of fields in our own age of information. Knowledge and insight mean power. The control of this power creates the possibility for a few "chosen" ones. The diffusion of knowledge and insight means, for some, the loss of their power and control. This is the end of the elite.

All of us know this. All of us are tempted to play this game.

And yet the control of the masters is constantly under threat. It happens all the time when people realize that they can do for themselves what was always done for them. Even sacrosanct powers like the juridical and medical world are becoming "protestantized."

There is the case of the patient who asks her clinic to diagnose her. She gets the results, reads up on the illness, examines the different possible medications, checks on a computer on side-effects, and gets the medicine needed on her own or with the help of her doctor. Maybe it's an extreme case, but not an unknown one.

The world of DIY (Do It Yourself) and self-help indicates that people are reclaiming initiatives that had been taken over from them. This is happening in practically all fields. We are freer than we think!

And yet we have a long way to go. During recent elections in India a woman was asked by an American journalist for whom she was voting. She answered that she had never been told that she could vote.

In a smilar vein, Elizabeth Dreyer, professor in spirituality at the Washington Theological Union, argues that "ordinary" Christians are rarely made aware of their own spiritual dimensions in a world where holiness, mysticism, charism, and prayer are considered the qualities of the professional saint, the priest, the nun or monk. Ordinary examples of everyday sanctity and asceticism seem almost always overlooked. Millions are kept away from their own gifts and powers because they are kept ignorant and embezzled, poor and uninformed.

This secrecy is not the way of Jesus. He never intimidates anyone, He makes it clear that everyone is plugged in on the divine power line.

"I have spoken openly to all the world. ... I have said nothing in secret" (Jn 18:20). He did not point to his message with a warning: High voltage, don't touch! On the contrary, he refers to it as a lamp that must not be hidden (Lk 8:17).

One day when I was working in Nairobi, Kenya, the Headmaster of the Dutch Primary School contacted me. He told me that he himself was an agnostic; he doubted any religious dimension. Nevertheless, he asked me whether I would be willing to give some religious classes to the children of his school.

What made his request all the more surprising was that the school he was running was a type of school called in the Netherlands a *public* (*Openbare*) school. It is a school where no religion is taught. It is a school that is constitutionally protected by the Dutch law to offer nonbelieving parents a school that respects their nonbelief—a right that needed protection in that once-staunchly Christian country.

I listened to his request, but told him it would not be possible. His school could not permit something like that. He answered that he knew that. He even added that he himself was opposed to the whole idea, but that the parents insisted that some religion be taught. And as those same parents themselves were paying him his salary, and not the Dutch state, he felt he must respect their wishes. In most cases the parents were not believers either. Yet they had all urged him to find someone who could give their children some religious instruction.

He gave me two reasons. One was that if those Dutch children didn't hear the Bible stories in school, they would never hear them. This is a difficulty that doesn't exist for children as long as they live in the Netherlands. They would practically always hear them in one way or another. But in Kenya they would never hear them. They would loose contact with their own Dutch Judeo-Christian cultural roots.

There was a second reason, based on a frightening experience they had heard of. All too often in the circle of their friends and acquaintances, youngsters had come into contact with one or another strange guru who had introduced them to the divine dimension in themselves, and led them off to become Hare Krishna devotees, or Divine Child adherents, or members of a fundamentalist sect. So their request was that I introduce those kids to Bible stories, to prayer, and make them aware of their own spiritual dimension.

Those parents understood, though in an oblique way, that this dimension should not remain hidden from their children. But even in an ecclesiastical clerical context this often happens. Our own spiritual gifts and potential remain hidden and are sometimes even denied. Too often we are supposed to rely merely on others.

But it is not only the powers that be, who should be blamed. Too many of us are unwilling to take up the challenge of God's love. We resist its grace. We do not want to be "connected" to the life from heaven; we do not want to be "taken up."

Someone who has explored this issue is M. Scott Peck, the psychiatrist whose book, *The Road Less Traveled*, has been on the *New York Times* bestseller list for almost seven years. He explains that very few choose this "less-traveled road," although it becomes clear to them during psychiatric treatment that it is the only way toward genuine human health and maturity.[23] Scott Peck thinks that there are two reasons for this: too many people are afraid of the power it would give them, and of the responsibility involved. In a word, they are afraid of their own depths.

It is not only of their own depths that they are afraid, but of that still point deep within them where they would find God and God's love and energy.

Loved by God, we are destined to love with God's love in us.

The consequences of this love are the theme of the novels of Andrew M. Greeley, priest, sociologist, and one of the most prolific and widely-read authors in this country. He describes in many ways the passionate "love affair" that God has with each one of God's creatures.

In his novels, God is variously seen as Father, Mother, Spouse, Friend, Knight, Brother, Sister, and Friend. It is that divine love we meet when we experience any love in our lives. It is that love with which we ourselves are "charged." God's love is in us. We should drink from the breasts of God our loving Mother.[24] God discloses Godself through the order and the inviting attractiveness of creation. It is a love that, were it better known, could change the world, for it is a love that embraces all of us.

Which brings us to another difficult question: What then is love?

The debate on this question has raged for ages, with every kind of distinction having been offered. The names for these distinctions are so old that they are often rendered in classical Greek: *eros*, *philia*, *agape*, as well as "platonic love," and so forth. So many definitions have been set forth, yet they all seem inadequate. Love remains a mystery.

John, who called himself the beloved disciple of Jesus, would agree. Of course love is a mystery: God is love.

It is in his first letter that John gives a summary of his understanding of love. Considering his close relationship to Jesus, it is possible to imagine that the two often discussed the subject. His summary states:

> My dear friends
> let us love each other,
> since love is from God
> and everyone who loves is a child of God
> and knows God,
> because God is love. (1 Jn 4:7-8)

This may sound lofty, abstract, and perhaps not terribly helpful. In fact, it is far from abstract.

It is God's love that gave us life, our greatest gift. Why God offered us this present remains a mystery—the mystery of God's love. And if God is with us we will find within ourselves the same life-giving dynamic.

The story of our creation, which is the story of God's life-giving acts, teaches us a lot about love. Even before human life was given *sustenance* and *nurture* were provided for. God first separated the land and the water; light was given, both for the day and for the night; the earth was filled with plants and animals, with fruits and flowers. And only after all this were human beings made. It is the same love that causes expectant parents to provide for the coming baby. I so often meet that type of love — God's providing love — in the people around me. I asked a class full of relatively poor children whether their parents loved them. They all said yes. I asked them, how do you know? There was a moment of utter silence. Then a small girl put up her hand and said: "They work so that I can eat." Another said, "My father puts me to bed and reads to me." And another, "My mother made this dress for me" — adding with a coy smile, "and she made it so pretty."

Once with one of my African students I visited his family upcountry. They had been warned of my coming. At our arrival his elderly father gave me a sheep to be eaten — by me, during my stay in the family! His mother offered me some tea. I noticed then that the water for that tea came from a canister my friend had been carrying all the way from where our car had stopped at the end of the road. The water I was going to drink was water brought from the city. He had been afraid that I would get sick from the well water they were using at his home. *Providing love!*

But love is not only a question of providing what is needed. It is not only life, but the quality of life that counts, too: the packing it comes in, the decorations, the colors, the sounds, and the music.

God did not just give us plants and fruits to eat — but pineapples and tomatoes, plums and strawberries, lemons and oranges, cherries and coconuts.

It was not only the blue of the sky that was given, but also the greens and the reds, purple and yellow, indigo and grey: all signs of care and love, of respect and friendship.

Beyond the provisions for our material survival we need emotional support. We need security, affection, recognition, admiration, the feeling of being wanted, needed, and appreciated.

After the creation of the human being, after the provision for all the material needs, that story too is part of the creation story. The tale is told twice, each in a different way, but the two stories should be told together. They complement each other.

In the second story we are created woman and man, both in the image of God. But there is the earlier story in which one human being is created. God leads that one being—the human being—through the whole of the earth, showing everything provided for, and asking "it" to name everything it sees.

The narration makes it clear that this intellectualizing and theorizing activity does not prevent the human being from feeling terribly bored. There is no emotional support from an equal. Life is unbearable. God, too, notices this. So God divides the one into two.

It is at the moment when these two human beings see the whole of reality reflected in one another's eyes that human love is born. And as they only have eyes for each other, God discretely leaves them alone, only visiting now and then in the afternoon, when the cool of the evening wind has refreshed them all.

That is the way God provided our emotional support from the very beginning.

We are God's gifts to each other.

But the way God provides for our needs is not the only way we learn about God's love and what this loves works in us.

God remains faithful, even when we fail to live up to that reality, even when we offer one another not a gift but a threat. God listens to the oppressed and intervenes on their behalf. We have encountered this theme in a story like Exodus, when

Moses was inspired to empower and liberate his people.

This is a reality that is with us in the darkness and desolation of our own days. The voice of God's protest is again and again awakened among us, even in our own indignation when we hear about injustice and oppression. It is a voice that never will be silenced. It is a fact of life.

In November 1989 six Jesuits and their cook and her daughter were murdered on the campus of the Central American University in San Salvador. Their crime was simple. They had protested against the exploitation of their neighbors. They had allowed themselves to be touched by the love God has for the poor and exploited campesinos in their country.

The forms of that exploitation are legion. There are so many ways we exploit others. Every time we use others for our gratification, we overlook their true status. We do not live according to the truth about them, about ourselves, and about God. We are not in touch with God's loving power in us, the love Luke calls "the Spirit of Jesus."

We are not attentive to reality. We do not see and we do not listen. We live a lie.

Scott Peck argues that the principal form that the work of love takes is *attention*.[25] When we love another person, we give him or her our attention, we attend to that person's reality. He adds that the most common and important way in which we can exercise our attention is by *listening*. God listens all through scripture and all through human history. God listens to everyone. God listens with special interest to those whom nobody else listens to, to those whose divine origin and nature is overlooked and neglected. It is what God did in ancient Egypt. It is what God does all the time. It is God's preferential love for the exploited.

When God's love for humanity and creation is in us, we are facing quite a program. We are carriers of an energy we hardly ever tap in our everyday life. Yet the energy is there. It is there almost as something we only remember from the past. It is a love we should remember in view of our future and the Kingdom of God to come. We live in what some of us would call a "time warp." It is the kind of time warp T.S. Eliot may have had in mind when he wrote, "And the end of all our exploring will be to arrive where we started, and know the place for the first time."

Chapter Seven

Remembering the Future

In 1969 I finally went to Africa to teach philosophy and religious studies at the University of Nairobi, at that time the only university in Kenya. That journey changed my whole life. I was entering an old culture that was entirely new to me. Everything—life, death, sickness, health—was interpreted in ways I was not accustomed to.[26] So was "time."

In those days a discussion was going on among my African colleagues about the question of "time." Professor John Mbiti, one of the preeminent theologians of East Africa, had just published a study entitled *New Testament Eschatology in an African Background.*[27] In that book he studied the idea of time among his people, the Akamba. His conclusion was that for this people—and for all the other African peoples he had studied—time is a two-dimensional phenomenon, a distant past and a dynamic present; the future, he argued, is virtually non-existent.

> Time as a succession or simultaneity of events "moves" not forward but backward. People look more to the "past" for the orientation of their being than to anything that might yet come into human history. For them history does not move towards any goal yet in the future: rather, it points to the roots of their existence, such as

60

the origin of the world, the creation of man, the formation of their customs and traditions, and the coming into being of their whole structure of society.[28]

The future is the memory of the past.[29] To give a simple example: I know that it will be a market day this coming Wednesday, because it has been a market day on Wednesdays in the past as long as I can remember.

Many of Mbiti's African colleagues disagreed with him passionately. They thought it a betrayal of the African cause. How could a respected African scholar hold that Africans didn't know about a "future"?

It is not my intention to enter that discussion. But at the time it clarified something in my mind I had never understood before.

I remember how one day, as a teenager, sick in bed, recovering from the effects of famine in the Netherlands toward the end of the Second World War, I was caught by the idea that it should be possible to know the future as well as the past. I thought that if I really entered into myself I would be able to connect with my future — not with the details, but definitely with my general development and growth. In other words I thought that I would be able to trace in broad outlines what — to use a familiar expression — life would have in store for me. That expression itself seems to point at the tension we confronted in the preceding chapter. It points at what we sometimes call nowadays a "time warp." Everything is already there. All is in store, and at the same time it not yet there, as it still has to be brought into the light of day. It is the stress and suspense we find in a seed; the whole plant is in the seed already, and yet it still has to develop and grow.

You can put the problem in a philosophical way. What is time? Does time exist for God? Of course not, when you come to think about it. For God the whole of time is present in one eternal moment. The future is a working out, a clarifying or actualization of that eternal moment in God. Something that in reality already exists comes into the light of day. Consequently there is a kind of tension between where we are and the reality of what will be.

This might sound mysterious. Yet I think it explains a lot of things. Take the familiar biblical saying where Jesus declares himself to be the light of the world. What does this mean? Does it mean that he brings something new into this world? I think not. That is not what light does. Light does not bring anything new. Light reveals things that were not seen before.

Just imagine having an old house with a loft. That loft is hardly ever visited. It is too high and too difficult to reach. Over the years all kinds of things were stored in the loft. One day you decide to inspect it. You take a flashlight, pull down the trapdoor, climb the creaking steps of the ladder, and find yourself in the dark. A sticky spider web falls over your face. You switch on your light and suddenly, in that light, you see what is in the loft: old books and paintings, toys and furniture, phonograph records, old pieces of clothing. Your light does not bring anything new; it shows you what is there.

In the light of Jesus our own content and treasure lights up. We see the difference between how we are now and how we are destined to be. It is a light that causes in us the tension between the present, the future, and all that was and has been stored in us from the very beginning.

There are many gospel analogies that play with the same idea: the difference between the smallest of seeds and the fully grown tree; between the pinch of yeast and the leavened loaf; between the Kingdom that is at the same time already here and that remains not-yet.

You find the same kind of suspense when Jesus compares the Kingdom of God to a treasure or a pearl that is hidden. The treasure is already there, and so is the pearl—but they are not yet found.

According to Luke, before Jesus leaves his disciples he gives them a task, a mission. He says, "Go out and bear witness of me even in the farthest corners of the earth" (Acts 4:32-35).

In the Gospel according to Matthew the same mission is given in other words. The disciples must announce to everyone on earth that we relate to a Father, a Son, and a Holy Spirit (Mt 28:19). In other words, they have to tell everyone that they originate from God, that they are God's offspring, and that they all live by God's Spirit. They not only have to announce that; they have to initiate others into that truth by baptism.

Again we meet the same kind of dynamics. Announcing this message and baptizing believers does not bring them anything new; rather, it reveals their true nature.

In my earlier days as a missionary I thought that someone became a child of God at the moment he or she heard about the trinitarian formula and wanted to be baptized. That is obviously not true. We are children of God before we hear about any special theorem. When Jesus uses the terms Father, Son, and Spirit in relation to us, he is not expressing a hope or a desire. *He is stating a fact.*

We are born from God, created in God, and vivified by God. Baptism is an initiation rite. We use the term initiation rite for baptism, confirmation, the eucharist, and marriage without too much difficulty. I, too, used to use the word without much attention. Only when I was confronted with initiation rites in the African context did their meaning become clearer to me.

In Africa, boys and girls at marriageable age are not initiated into adult life to make them men or women. They are men and women at the moment of their initiation. Their initiation formalizes that fact for the initiates themselves, and for their community. An initiation rite does not give something new. It formalizes an existing reality.

Being baptized does not make us into God's children. That is what we are. Baptism makes this relationship into a formally recognized one. Nothing new, as such, is given.

When we are "commissioned" to announce this truth to others, we are not only informing them about their dignity, but at the same time we are informing ourselves about who we are. Everyone, to the ends of the earth, is my equal. And that is the truth.

The treasure we find in ourselves, namely that we are loved and named by God, is true of every human being we meet in our lives. It is as true of them as it is of us.

It is difficult to accept this, the fact that God loves others in the same way God loves us. It was difficult for the people in Nazareth during the Sabbath meeting described by Luke. It remains difficult for all of us.

One day during a workshop, as I explained this point about God's equal love for all, I noticed that one of the participants reacted strongly. She came to me afterwards to apologize. She told me what had happened to her. She was a religious who went twice a week from her convent to visit her sick mother at the other side of town. Driving to her mother, she always avoided a street that was known for its rowdy character. Everyone had warned her that if anything happened to her in that street she would really be in trouble.

One morning she was leaving the convent for her usual trip to her mother and she was really in an "alleluia" mood, convinced of God's love. Nothing could happen to her. That is why she decided to take the street she always avoided. As she went down the street a car with some youngsters came out of a side street and bumped into her car. There were further complications and she eventually had to appear in court.

But all that was not the real problem. Her real problem was her prayer to God after the accident: "How did you allow this to happen to me? To me, who has been faithful to you all my life? To me, on the very day when I was filled with praise for you? How could you allow those bums to drive into me?"

Realizing that God loves all people equally made her suddenly understand the nastiness hidden in her prayer.

To be true to yourself is quite a task. Our genuine self is rooted in the past, in our divine origin. It shows itself in the present, and it is going to be revealed further in our future. The tension that moves us forward, and that keeps us longing, is seated in the difference we experience between that "original" fact and our actual realization of it.

We find this disparity not only in relation to ourselves, but also in our relationship to others. We do not yet treat others as our equals. We do not yet pay sufficient attention to the plight of others. We have not yet been listening enough to our own situation.

When the murdered Jesuit Ignacio Ellacuría was buried in El Salvador in November 1989 his eulogist said that he was killed because of the part of the truth he had discovered *and* disclosed. He had listened to the exploited in his country, he had rendered that service of love, and he had had the courage to tell publicly what he had heard and seen. He died as a modern martyr, a contemporary witness to God's attentive love!

He also proved that what he did is possible for a human being. That is an important reality. It proves that a life that stands in contrast to the values of this world is not simply a dream. It demonstrates that God's love does break through in the life of a person who is truly attentive. That possibility shatters the pretexts we construct when we insist on the need to be realistic and rational, on the necessity of taking the world as it is, on the claim that there is nothing we can do about the way things are.

Every time a human being breaks a record or sets a new level of achievement something happens to us all. When we look at the performance of a top athlete we see the potential of our own bodies. When the first human being landed on the moon, in a sense we all shared in that accomplishment.

This is also true in the moral order of things. I experienced this when, as a child, I helped smuggle ration cards for hidden

Jewish families. In a world where the majority closed their ears out of fear and for all kinds of rational reasons, others did listen. So listening was possible.

I myself was hardly involved, as I was too young to understand, as the adults did, all the implications of what was going on.

> The lesson of the Holocaust is the facility with which most people, put into a situation that does not contain a good choice ... argue themselves away from the issue of moral duty ... adopting instead the precepts of rational interest and self-preservation.
>
> *In a system where rationality and ethics point in different directions, humanity is the main loser.* ... And there is another lesson of the Holocaust of no lesser importance. ... The second lesson tells us that putting self-preservation above moral duty is in no way predetermined, inevitable, and inescapable. One can be pressed to it, but one cannot be forced to it, and thus one cannot really shift the possibility of doing it on those who exerted the pressure. It does not matter how many people chose moral duty over the rationality of self-preservation—*what does matter is that some did.*[30]

The description of this achievement is described in terms of a moral duty. It is love, our attention to the reality of those others, that is at the base of these decisions.

When Jesus lived out his life among us, he broke all existing boundaries—and in a sense, all rules—once and for all. He projected an alternative world, lived by himself in his own life.

By showing us and sharing with us his life, he put the whole of humanity in the tension between who we are now, and who we will be at the moment we live God's love for ourselves, for others, for the world, and the universe. It is that tension that explains the dynamic of love within each one of us. All that Jesus realized among us continues to draw his community to respond fully to God's love and attention. And he left us the memory of what he meant in the breaking of the bread and the sharing of the wine. The eucharistic celebration, during which we thank God for our existence, commemorates him and his risen life among us.

At the same time, the Eucharist sets us on the way to a future we have to build. During its celebration we realize sacramentally the one body of Christ we do not yet manage to realize in the concreteness of our everyday life.

Every time this celebration occurs we experience the tension between the past, the present, and the future. We remember now what happened before in view of the future to come. Our future is bound up with that past. Celebrating the Eucharist we go back to a past that we have to turn into our future. It is not without reason that the Eucharist is often called "Mass," or mission. We are on a mission.

It is not only Christians who are thus drawn. The "suspense" between who we are now and who we are called to be, draws all of humanity.

The whole of humanity, the whole of creation is clamoring to be who and what it really is. We feel a glory in us that has not yet been realized. That drawing power and the tension it creates is the heart of all our concerns and hopes. It is the origin of any revolution and reform. It is, when thwarted and frustrated, at the core of depression and addiction. It is behind the urge to do scientific work, and the reason for the success of books on self-healing. It explains the search of the New Age believer and the untiring creativity of the artist. It is the treasure and presence sought in prayer and meditation. It is the loneliness of the unloved, the longing for wholeness in all of us, the reaching out to the other. It is life and existence itself. It is the lover waiting at the window. It explains the cry of the child at birth, and the sigh of the elder who dies.

It is the hope that there is *Someone* who listens and hears all, who will neither forget nor forsake us. It is the tension between the past, and the future in the present. It is our trust in Jesus and our impatience with so much that is organized and done in his name.

It is the gist of our constant yearning for a redeeming alternative.

Chapter Eight

Sincerely Yours: Sharing All Things

Luke has preserved a particularly vivid description of the earliest Christian communities. In fact, he is so enthusiastic that he repeats himself. Here is the prototype of what God's love does to people:

> Those who accepted his message were baptized, and about three thousand were added to their number that day. They devoted themselves to the apostles' teaching and to the fellowship, to the breaking of bread and to prayer. Everyone was filled with awe, and many wonders and miraculous signs were done by the apostles. All the believers were together and had everything in common. Selling their possessions and goods, they gave to anyone as he had need. Every day they continued to meet together in the temple courts. They broke bread in their homes and ate together with glad and sincere hearts, praising God and enjoying the favor of all the people. And the Lord added to their number daily those who were being saved. (Acts 2:42-47)
>
> The whole company of believers was united in heart and soul. Not one of them claimed any of his possessions

as his own; everything was held in common. With great power the apostles bore witness to the resurrection of the Lord Jesus, and all were held in high esteem. There was never a needy person among them, because those who had property in land or houses would sell it, bring the proceeds of the sale, and lay them at the feet of the apostles, to be distributed to anyone in need. (Acts 4:32-35).

In fact, it was this new spirit that attracted Luke to these communities and got him interested in Jesus.

Of course, Luke is not only good at describing those who are willing to share. He is also expert in depicting the rich person who is unwilling to share what he has acquired. In one of Jesus' parables a wealthy farmer reflects, "I will say to myself, 'You have plenty of good things laid by, enough for many years to come: take life easy, eat, drink and enjoy yourself'" (Lk 12:21).

It is in the stark opposition between two contrasting attitudes that we can understand Luke's Beatitudes and their parallel Woes. The text is from Jesus' so-called Sermon on the Plain. If these are not his exact words, they may certainly be regarded as a summary of Jesus' teaching.

Blessed are you who are poor, for yours is the Kingdom of God.

Blessed are you who hunger now, for you will be satisfied. Blessed are you who weep now, for you will laugh.

Blessed are you when men hate you, when they exclude you and insult you and reject your name as evil, because of the Son of Man.

Rejoice in that day and leap for joy, because great is your reward in heaven. For that is how their fathers treated the prophets.

But woe to you who are rich, for you have already received your comfort.

Woe to you who are well fed now, for you will go hungry. Woe to you who laugh now, for you will mourn and weep.

Woe to you when all men speak well of you, for that is how their fathers treated the false prophets. (Lk 6:20–27)

It should not be thought that Jesus is here idealizing poverty or implying that anyone should be in need or poor. Jesus knew the horrors of the poor of his time. He was constantly summoned by them, blind beggars in the street gutters, helpless lepers in the shade of some trees outside of the townships, a raving madman living amidst the pigs in a cemetery. In his day, as in our own, poverty meant misery, no access to education, medical care, or security. Jesus could not have been in favor of that. The very first act of love is — as we have noted — to provide what is needed.

What Jesus does is tell us that we should share our goods in such a way that poverty is banished from the world.

The rich person goes wrong when he refuses to share in that fundamental fight against poverty, when he only thinks of himself and about taking life easy.

Some familiar examples of ownership and the use of property will help us understand what may go wrong.

— A farmer walks over his land, sowing his seeds. He turns abruptly at the point where his land borders on the land of his neighbor.

— A pioneer steps from his horse after a long and exhausting journey. He drives four poles in the earth to claim the land on which he plans to build his house.

— In the evening, the trader counts the gain of the day and puts it aside.

That is how property often works. *A piece is cut out of the whole and reserved for one or some alone.* I put my money in a bank account. There it mixes with the money of others, though it remains my part. If I invent something, or write a book, I claim a patent or copyright. If it is something really useful that I have found, then there is even more reason to take this precaution. After all, there may be money in it.

We do all that we can to protect what we have from the rest. Our right to do so is well established, and guaranteed by our legal system, backed up police, and even insured by our right to own personal weapons.

One Christmas night I was asked to assist in a suburban parish. The pastor asked me whether I would like to stay overnight. I did not. I knew that he had a loaded gun next to his bed to defend himself, if need be, against thieves. Suppose I had to find the bathroom during the night and he, in his sleep, were to forget that he had a guest and shoot at my shadow, in order to protect his property.

Property rights—that is, *the right to take a part of the whole for oneself*—are so well protected, so ingeniously organized that increasingly more effort is spent on the protection of that part and less on the whole.

A simple example of this process can be seen in an index published in January 1990. The income tax of the richest one percent of American families went down by fifteen percent since 1980, while over the same period the income tax of the poorest twenty percent of American families went up by nineteen percent.

There is an almost unavoidable relation between riches and power. That is not only true of the one who possesses material goods or money; it is also true of the one who "owns" knowledge and education, expertise and skills, prestige and the right connections.

Power is not necessarily wrong, though in a gospel context it remains a delicate issue. The "subversive conspiracy between power and riches, which Jesus names mammon,"[31] is not an unavoidable outcome, though it is the usual one in the world as it is currently structured.

In an alternative world it would not be like that.

Jesus was the most powerful personality anyone could

hope to meet. He was so powerful because he was so "rich." It is in the use of power that the devil — symbol for all evil in the world — came to test him in the desert. How was he going to use it? For himself alone?

Jesus was immensely endowed in his personal gifts, his insights, his connections with God, his knowledge, his influence over people, and so many other charisms manifested during his life. He did not dispense with his powers, nor did he use them to enrich himself personally. He used them in the service of the Kingdom of God, to serve others, to enrich them through his sharing. His power was a blessing to us. Our power could be a blessing to others, too. If we are of Jesus' spirit, that is how it should be.

In 1986 when the Catholic Bishops of the United States published their statement, "Economic Justice for All: Catholic Social Teaching and the U.S. Economy," the reaction of many affluent Catholics was rather negative. Meetings were organized to address those apprehensions. The featured speaker at one such meeting was the Archbishop of Milwaukee, Rembert G. Weakland.

As Weakland climbed the podium to address the audience, the tension in the hall was palpable. He began by explaining why a church committed to the Kingdom of God here on earth was interested in the wealthy. He said, "You are rich, and that means that you have power." He challenged them because of their power. And they understood.

The first time I met Americans who had accepted this challenge was in Nairobi. A group of Americans had heard me preach at the university chapel and they invited me to meet with them. They explained that they belonged to a Christian community in Washington, D.C., the Church of the Savior. (Little did I know at that time that I would one day live just a block away from that community in Washington.)

In that community they had formed an action group called "Ministry of Money." It is rare to find money mentioned in such an up-front manner in a Christian context, and I immediately found myself quite interested in that group. When they explained themselves, I became even more intrigued. They told me that when anyone joins their community, they must follow a particular procedure.[32] The new candidate is asked to attend a retreat in a farm/conference center owned by the community not far from the city: the Dayspring Retreat Farm. In that quiet setting they try to discover what "talent" the candidate brings to the community. Those personal gifts vary greatly — from cooking to writing, from nursing to gardening, from peacemaking to praying. The members are subsequently asked to participate — using that particular personal gift — in the numerous and diverse tasks and missions the community sets for itself.

In some cases the gift is money. Some people are very rich, and as a result they enjoy great influence in the world. They may be major shareholders in a company or serve as directors and managers. Can this "giftedness" be used in the service of the Kingdom? That is the issue to which the group is trying to respond, and that was the theme they asked me to address.

I no longer remember exactly what I told them. I do remember, however, a discussion about how many millions of dollars are spent in pharmaceutical research on the diseases, cosmetic needs, and other discomforts of the rich, while the diseases of the poor in the world remain neglected.

If bilharzia — a debilitating and deadly parasitical disease — were rampant in the so-called First World, it would definitely receive the urgent attention of the leading pharmaceutical firms. The first serious anti-malaria research in this country started when American soldiers had to survive in the tropics. If the rich have any influence in decision making in this field, they should definitely use it.

Any gift we have is not given to us for our personal enjoyment. This truth was a topic for debate among Jesus and his apostles. They frequently tell him — just as Satan in the desert did — to use his talents to enrich himself, to get promoted, to be honored, in the hope that they will be able to share in that money, that honor, and that glory.

With every miracle they get excited at its promotional, managerial, and commercial potential. All the while Jesus is excited about the possibility his gifts offer for the service of others, to liberate them from the evil that threatens them and the whole world.

Jesus refuses to set himself and what he has apart from the rest. He engages it in the "wholeness" of God's creation.

Property can only be a constructive factor in our spiritual growth when it is actively relating to, and engaged in that "wholeness." In other words, it is only valid when it serves the cause of what is true and right. God loves all of us equally, and God provided this world equally for all of us. The bottom line is that it all remains God's property, provided in view of all creation.

Any property we own is really God's gift. It is God's. Nothing is really ours without any further ado. There is always that further ado. Pope John Paul II boils it down to one simple core principle: "The goods of the world are meant for all."[33]

That rule applies to all I own; all property should be seen in that light. As soon as my possessions are separated by me for myself alone, apart from the rest, my property becomes something sick and perverse. It is like a malignant tumor growing ever larger.

The point is not that we have no personal needs or any right to private property. The point, as John Paul II clearly states in his encyclical, *On Social Concern*, is that this private property exists under a "social mortgage." It has to be referred and related to the whole of the human community. Or, to say it the way Pope Paul VI did: "Every person has the right to get what he or she needs from the earth; all other rights must be subordinate to this."[34] What we own beyond our needs has to be related to those rights of everyone.

How then should we own?

In the way that Jesus does. How does Jesus own? In view of the service of everyone. That is what his "poverty" is about.

It does not mean that he went without food and drink, rest and sleep, clothing and sandals, or even without parties and picnics. But in the end, all this was used for the service of all.

He never owned anything in the way the rich man in the beginning of this chapter did. When God gave that man the bountiful gift of a rich harvest, he built barns to store it all for himself, saying, "You have plenty of good things laid by, enough for many years to come. Take life easy, eat, drink, and enjoy yourself." He was rich in his own eyes, but a pauper in the sight of God.

This applies not only to the possession of material goods. It is also true of friendship, relationships, information, skills and technical know-how, as well as our spiritual power, charisms, and gifts.

After having related the sad end of the stupidly rich man, Jesus goes on, in Luke's text, to say how we should *be* and how we should *own*.

We should be like a beautiful flower, gifted with color and fragrance that just stands there, giving away all it has to the world around, enriching our lives, pleasing our senses (Lk 12:22–34). We should *be* and *live* with all we have in view of all, like a flower in the sun, like the sun itself!

It is Luke who says, "Keep in mind the words of the Lord Jesus, who himself said: 'Happiness lies more in giving than in receiving'" (Acts 20:35). We should use what we have to make friends (Lk 19:9). We should invest wisely in "heaven," that is, the Reign of God (Lk 12:33).

The opposite of this attitude can be illustrated by the rich banker who some time ago bought a painting of some sunflowers by Van Gogh for $35 million in order to have it for himself, to withdraw it from the rest of us, to whom God gave this artist and his talent.

Nowhere in the gospel is it said that these lessons are easy for the rich and affluent. On the contrary. Jesus speaks about the eye of a needle through which the rich must pass (Lk

28:25). Even if we don't take this saying literally, the difficulty remains. We have to travel lighter.

On average an American consumes about 22 tons of material per year, twice as much as the Japanese, ten times the world average.[35] The same average American produces 1200 pounds of garbage a year. That is an average of 3.5 pounds a day, or around 100 pounds per month, twice as much garbage as the average Japanese or West German.[36] If all humans in the world were to match this wasteful standard the planet would quickly become exhausted and uninhabitable.

As Tom McGrath has written,

Every bag of groceries I bring home or bag of trash I take out to the alley has an effect halfway around the world. For the goods of the world to be available to all, one thing is certain — to be moral the lives of Americans have to change. My life has to change. And to change is hard when you're loaded down with more than your share of the world's goods.[37]

The gospel message is clear: we are asked not only to give what we have as alms for the poor; we have to claim less for ourselves of what is available for our personal use, and invest what is left in such a way that it is helpfully shared with those who are poor.

Again, the statistics on what we affluent Christians spend on ourselves are staggering. Though Christians number only 32% of the world population, they receive 62% of the entire world's income and spend 97% of it on themselves.[38]

Even if we were willing to give up our selfishness and invest what we have and who we are in the service of others, would such an alternative approach be possible in the world as currently structured? Would a Christian community like the one described by Luke in the Acts of the Apostles be feasible in our time?

Certainly we are not all going to sell all goods, stocks and shares, and distribute the proceeds to the poor. Heroic and saintly as that would be, it is not a solution to our problem—nor was it for the early Christians! The challenge is not to do something *for* the poor—an attitude that smacks of the worst elements of paternalism. The task is to be *with* the poor, which involves standing alongside them and helping them to develop their own resources and power to the point that they may become the subjects of change.[39]

There are, however, some other obstacles to be overcome. The first one relates to what we mentioned in our chapter on "The People of God." As long as we keep on restricting our religious life to what is going on in the church and in its sanctuary it will remain impossible to visualize seriously any plan for realizing the Kingdom outside of the sanctuary.

In a way we are facing here the same difficulty the Pharisees (and consequently Jesus) were experiencing with the temple service of their time. The Pharisees were upset about the priestly temple service of their time because it had become something on its own without any direct reference to the justice and mercy to be realized by and among the people of God. They did not find in the temple service anything that reminded them of the exodus event.

I am not questioning that the Eucharist should be the center of our lives. It certainly should. But not in the way we often celebrate it. The Eucharist only makes sense when we are willing to realize the true meaning of that sacrifice, the breaking of the body and the sharing of the blood, in our concrete everyday world.

The worship of God cannot stand alone and apart. There is the wider issue of wholeness and healing. The breaking of the bread, the sharing of the wine, the weaving and building of his body, is something that has to be operative in a world that is polarized between North and South, between the ever-more rich and the ever-more poor. We are called to share in Christ's sacrifice, yes, but so that we can share in his wholeness and his healing mission.

We should celebrate as an effective response to our own and the world's longing for the Kingdom of God. That longing is evident through the world, on the part of individuals as well as great assemblies of people, clamoring for healing and wholeness.

The issues that bring people together may be different in front of the Capitol building, around the Lincoln Memorial, in Wenceslas Square in Prague, in front of the cathedral in Bogota, in the streets of Soweto in South Africa, in Tienanmen Square in Beijing, and in the refugee camps of Hong Kong or Ethiopia. But the demands are the same: heal this world, give us our rights, chase away the evil spirits of tyranny and domination, let us leave the past, respect our dignity, allow us to build a more human and divine world.

As long as we in our Christian communities separate the sacred from the profane, reserving one part to some and the rest to others, the issue will not be solved. As long as we maintain an inequality in our hearts, there will be those who have and those who have not, the rich and the poor. The world will not be saved, because we do not share in common, and cannot sit together as equals to discuss how we are going to invest ourselves and all we have in God's Kingdom among us.

That brings us to another condition that has to be met. It has something to do with prophecy. Not prophecy in the sense of foretelling the future, but prophecy that interprets contemporary events in light of the will of God.

Before we begin investing our property, our expertise, skills, and other "talents," we should critically examine the structures we meet in this world. We should examine their intentions and aims. Do they really contribute to God's Kingdom in this world, or do they promote the worship of false gods? Do those structures allow us to realize our aims?

In his encyclical *On Social Concern* Pope John Paul II denounced both "Marxist collectivism" and "liberal capitalism." He explained that both of them harbor a tendency toward oppressive imperialism—heavily loaded terms.

We can say it in a less technical way. Neither communism nor capitalism can, according to the pope, help us any further on the way to the realization of God's love among us.

We have to be more attentive, we have to listen better to those we would like to serve. We have to listen better to those who are called blessed by Jesus.

He calls them blessed because they will help us further to share in such a way that poverty might be banished from the world and so that the *Spirit of Jesus* in us will penetrate all the areas of our work and life.

The poor are the ones who have real *authority* in this world. We should listen to them *obediently*.

Chapter Nine

Obediently Yours: Listening to Whom?

One day when I was a boy one of my sisters came home in great consternation. Her teacher, who was a nun, had informed the class that she would be leaving that very night. Tomorrow they would have another teacher. My sister was terribly upset because she loved her teacher, as did many other children as well. No one knew why she was being transferred, but the class knew how she had found out about her new appointment because she told them.

Upon returning to her room, the day before, she had found a railway ticket with her new destination. There was a note which contained only the hour and date of her departure. She knew what it meant: a new appointment to another convent and school in another town.

That is what obedience often meant in those days. Perhaps it is an extreme case; some might even suspect it is a caricature. Yet, that is how things went. In a way, it was even held up as the ideal.

During my novitiate we were introduced to the lives of saints who practiced the same kind of blind obedience. We were encouraged to read the stories of saints in the desert who tried, in the spirit of obedience to their superiors, to perform such feats as carrying water in a basket.

Most likely there was some merit in such exercises—especially as both parties must have known that something more was at stake than simply fetching water. Perhaps there was at play a subtle love for God and for each other.

But of course my sister could hardly have appreciated such reasoning. She was terribly upset. It is quite likely that her teacher was much less affected. Certainly, she may have disliked the move, and she may well have disliked the way she was ordered about. But it was something foreseen and accepted in her life because of her love for Jesus. Because of that love she had made a vow of obedience.

But too often the obedience demanded in those days had little, apparently, to do with love. It was almost a giving away of one's responsibility—something that is less meritorious. As Jack Dominian notes,

> Those who enjoy the advantages of this counsel will speak of the inner freedom it gives, the proper ordering of their life, the strengthening of its meaning and peace. All this is possible, but it can also be a withdrawal from responsibility, an abdication of maturity and absence of inner direction.[40]

At its worst, this type of obedience is a perpetuation of a child-parent relationship—or worse, a slave to a master, an inferior to a superior—in a structure of dependence. Such an attitude can produce a kind of immaturity and infantilism that may do terrible damage to human integrity.

In the period of transition just after the Second Vatican Council, some priests in the Dutch diocese where I then lived and worked contacted the bishop and told him, "Just send us your instructions by mail and we will do exactly as you tell us to do." In other words: For heaven's sake, don't make us responsible!

History proves that blind obedience can and does cause

havoc. Many perpetrators of the Holocaust justified their behavior on the grounds that they were not responsible, that they were only following orders. But the courts did not find this excuse acceptable. For many, this verdict ended one period and opened up a new one whose watchwords were accountability and authenticity.

Of course, that didn't mean that obedience must disappear. Order of any sort requires obedience. The question is how obedience is to be understood.

The English word *obedience* comes from a Latin root, *obaudire*. At the center of that root is *audire*, to listen — hence audition, audio, and so forth. To obey means to *listen*, the activity which Scott Peck, as we have described, characterizes as the proof of love. To obey is to pay attention, to listen, to love.

So we have a listening that includes a doing. The word is not really heard if it is not acted upon: "Happy are those who listen to the word of God, and keep to it" (Lk 11:28).

To obey God is to listen to God, to be in the company of God. Like Jesus. All through his gospel Luke mentions how Jesus listens to the Father. Before any decision we find him praying. Thus, according to many traditional accounts, Jesus is the model of obedience.

Jesus obeyed his Father. Unfortunately, that obedience is often misunderstood. It is not understood in terms of the intimate love relationship between Jesus and his Father, but in terms of domination and submission: Jesus bent his will to the authority of his Father, just as we have so often to bend our will to someone else who has power over us.

When this is our model of the relationship between Jesus and his Father, then obedience means bending our will to the one with power. Thus, my sister's teacher had to do as she was told, whether she liked it or not, without any dialogue, negotiation, or even explanation.

Such a misunderstanding of obedience is common in religious life. As Aloysius Pieris notes,

Regrettably, we have invented another concept of obedience which is at variance with Yahweh's sovereignty: *hypotage* or submission, that is the ascetical practice of bending one's will to the "authority" (but in reality to the "power") of a human ruler, for example a religious superior, a bishop or pope, who claims to have a privileged contact with God by virtue of the institutional position he or she holds. But ... the New Testament always understands obedience as *hypakoe* (listening) and never as *hypotage* (ascetical submission).[41]

In a loving relationship this listening is something mutual. We all know this from our own experience. One of the most often-heard complaints in a relationship is the remark, "You never listen to me!"

God listens. God hears what is going on around us and within us. God hears the cries of everyone. God loves all equally and with the same kind of total abandon. And because of that impartial love God hears especially those who are oppressed, those who are marginalized and overlooked. *With God they have the greatest authority.* This is what the prophets have told us throughout the ages.

If we listen with God, we will hear what God hears. And we, too, will have to conclude that the wretched among us have the greatest authority.

That is what Luke tells us when he describes how Jesus ministers among the sick, the outcast, and the marginalized. Among the latter must be included women. In a time when pious men thanked God for not being born a woman, and did not speak publicly even with their wives and daughters, Luke pictures Jesus as surrounded with women who find in his company a new dignity and value.

When the angel announced to Mary in Nazareth that the child she would bear would be a Savior to the world, Mary knew intuitively what this would mean.

She had been listening long enough.

Upon meeting her aunt Elizabeth, she burst into song: "The poor will get their share!" (Lk 1:46–55).

Mary knew that a change in the world was needed because of the suffering of the poor. She had been listening with God.

There was a future to be realized by and for the whole of humanity. God's love for all would be realized. What was and is, would be. Mary remembered the future, promised by God to her forebears and described again and again by the prophets among her people. The world was going to change, evil would be overcome, and justice established.

We can express it in another way: *The poor among us are the ones who make a change in the world necessary.*

Any unwillingness on the part of the church or the world to listen to the cry of the poor and to change is a refusal to listen with God, to be in God's loving company.

Perhaps my reference to the authority of the poor is unclear. How could that homeless person on the street corner in Washington, D.C. have any authority over me? Why should I allow myself to be preached to by the hungry and poor in Latin America, or the half million homeless children in this country?

If I have been living with some attention to what is going on around me, then this question must have answered itself in my own life. And so it has.

There are moments when you have to listen, when you have no choice. I have often been in such situations, in circumstances where I had to listen, moments when I found myself confronted by true authority.

I recall the time when a student at the University of Nairobi sent for me to talk with him. I went to his room and he told me his story.

He had had a kind of infection on his leg for quite some time. He went to a doctor who gave him some antibiotics, which didn't really help. Then one day, as he was walking in town, he missed his step off the curb and his leg just snapped. In the hospital they told him that he had bone cancer. They amputated his leg. He returned to the university.

He had no choice but to return. His family had invested all their resources in him and his studies. *He* was going to be *their* entry to the modern world. But things had got worse. His lungs were affected.

Now he wanted to receive the sacrament of the sick. He said he knew he was going to die. He didn't mind that, he told me, but he did mind that his family would be so disappointed in him. He had been the only one they had been able to send to school. Because he was sent none of his brothers and sisters had been able to go. He had been their only hope, their real pride.

I listened. I had to listen. Would you not have listened? I heard the cry from within a society overlooked by the whole rest of the world, trying to survive in the midst of a hardship I could hardly imagine.

My heart cried with his, and I am sure God cried with us. *At that moment he was the suffering heart of the whole wide world,* the painful strain between what should have been and what it was. He was stretched over the length of that chasm as on a cross.

Such is the authority of the crucified.

I told him that I would come the next day for the anointing. No, he said, I could come to fetch him, for he would like to receive the last sacraments in the university chaplaincy.

Next morning he came to church. Some of his friends were with him. Afterwards I helped bring him with all his luggage (hardly anything at all) to a friend of his in town. I still remember how glad a small niece in that family was to see him. She danced and danced around him. He died some days later.

Listening to him brought back memories, the vision of prophets and dreamers. The meaning of Jesus' life echoes in you when you listen to a story like that. The vision and the realization of a different world, a more divine and human world. Story power is tremendous.

And there are so many stories to be told. Starvation in Ethiopia, drug abuse in Washington, D.C., exploitation in Latin America, sweatshops in South Korea, the red light district in Kowloon, a child abused in every corner of the world. It is in those sighs and groans that our small world opens up to the larger one, to the one where we are all loved by God, the world where we all belong together.

It would be intolerable to listen to all of them. It would overpower us. Yet listen we must, even before we think about what must be done. If we don't listen we might fail to fathom the depth, the length, and the intricacy of the roots of evil among us.

It is when we listen that those cries announce the future God is planning for the whole of humanity. It is when we listen that they speak with God's *authority*.

One rich man, Zacchaeus, discovered this. As Luke tells the tale, Zacchaeus was curious, but wealthy. That is why he counted himself out. It is Jesus who invites himself over to Zacchaeus's table. That is the reason that Zacchaeus hears the poor in the street say, "He has gone to a *sinner's* house as a guest."

Through his invitation Jesus opened a window in the heart of that wealthy man. He suddenly heard what those poor people said to him. He did not only hear it, he *listened* to what they were saying. And helped along by Jesus, who suggests that he can do it—*after all, isn't he, too, a son of Abraham?*—he does change and commit himself to a just and honest life.

Salvation is given because of the poor, the oppressed, those who suffer violence. It is a constant theme in Luke's gospel. God inclines to obey the summons of the neglected. In Jesus God makes their cry God's own. God wants to be our partner if we listen and obey.

Have we then to submit, to bend our will forcefully and ascetically to that authority because of God's power? If we take Jesus' obedience as our model, then a different approach comes into view. Jesus was not forced. He obeyed lovingly. He was the Father's equal. He was his Father's companion.

Neither does God force us. God's intervention in this world is of another order. God asks us in the person of Jesus to be attentive to the world around us, to listen, and to draw our conclusions.

I was once invited to take part in a discussion of Elie Wiesel's book *Night*, which is based on his experience as a prisoner in one of the Nazi death camps. In a well-known passage, Wiesel describes how he and his fellow prisoners were forced to watch the execution of two Jewish men and one young boy.

> The camp commander refused to serve as hangman. Three SS took over the job. Three necks were put into three nooses. ... "Where is God? Where is he?" said someone behind me. The three chairs were tipped over. ... We marched past ... the two men were no longer alive ... but the third rope was still moving. ... The child was lighter and was still living. Behind me I heard the same man ask "Where is God now?" and within me I heard an answering voice, "Where is he? Here he is— he hangs here on this gallows." In this night the soup had the taste of corpses.[42]

It seems that the author lost his faith in God. It hardly seems fair to discuss a reaction like that. The last word belongs to the victims, not to us. Yet, I was struck in our discussion by the comment of one of the participants: "God was there! But where were the ones who believed in God, where were *God's human companions?*"

Jesus asks us to be his companions. He does not want those who accept this invitation to be submissive like children, slaves, inferiors, or dependents. On the contrary, he calls them friends. He invites us to love as he does, to love as God loves. He asks us to accompany one another, as he himself is accompanying us.

He told his followers that among them there should be no master, that those distinctions should not be made.

> Among the gentiles, kings lord it over their subjects; and those in authority are given the title Benefactor. Not so with you: on the contrary, the greatest among you must bear himself like the youngest, the one who rules like the one who serves. . . . I am among you as a servant. (Lk 22:24–26)

He did not only say this. He lived it. Remember how he went that evening to the corner of the upper room, put off his upper garment, and stood in front of them with a towel over his shoulder, a container in his left hand and a pitcher of water in his right.

He put himself at the service of those whose feet he washed, placing them, their possibilities, their growth, their honor, and their glory, in the center of his own life.

He had authority over them, yes. But in the way linguists trace the term — going back to the original Latin root, *augere* — to increase, to make grow.

The people around him enjoyed being in his company. He was affirming, empowering, and life-giving. In the twenty-four chapters of his story of Jesus, Luke mentions twenty-two times how his coming brought great joy. People were transformed, healed, they felt themselves enriched, and started to radiate that joy themselves.

John the Baptizer immediately recognized him standing out in the crowd before him. Children flocked to him. Lepers were not afraid to hail him. Mary came forward to perfume his feet.

He brought people into contact who would not even have spoken to one another before: Samaritans, lepers, Greeks, Syro-Phoenecians, Romans. He opened their hearts to the poor, the blind lying in the gutters of the street, children, broken and abused men and women.

He helped all of them to bring their potential and possibilities, submerged in the dark depths of their inner lives, up to the surface and into the light of day.

Uncovering buried talents, healing atrophied gifts, making the blind to see, the deaf to hear, the lame to dance; stretching people beyond their limits; asking them to be his companions, to worship, sing, eat, drink, and dance with him; opening their minds, allowing a wider reading than in the past; putting all laws and regulations at the service of human persons, and their development and growth; and finally sharing responsibility with them, giving them his own— God's— Spirit.

The more you listen with God, the more you will be filled with God's compassion for those who are not heard, for those who are not respected; and the more you will be charged with God's love, the same love that made Jesus live his life and die his death, to rise to the new life.

This love is not just hanging in the air, pervading persons and things in some ethereal manner. It is love that has to be expressed in a human way, in a flesh and blood way, bodily, and *affectionately*.

Chapter Ten

Affectionately Yours:
Delight in Each Other

When Jesus was born in a stable in Bethlehem, his mother wrapped him in swaddling clothes (Lk 2:7). Those swaddling clothes tell us something about Luke's approach to what he discovered in the Christian communities. The reference to swaddling clothes (used twice by Luke) is sometimes taken as a sign of poverty or the lowly birth of Jesus. It is neither. It is a sign of what a caring Palestinian mother would do for her baby. It is a sign of Mary's maternal care.

You can almost smell the milk, the baby, the straw, the water over the fire, the swaddling clothes, the animals, the mother, and Joseph her beloved!

Luke has a keen eye for human details — more than any other evangelist. He gives us the details of Jesus' conception; he tells how neighbors and relatives streamed together to share the delight of Elizabeth and her voiceless husband Zechariah at the birth of their child, John.

He dwells at length on the story of Jesus' presentation in the temple, the detail about the two turtle-doves, and the old man Simeon who asked to be allowed to hold the child in his arms; and Anna, eighty-four years old, who for the rest of her life did not cease to talk about the child to anyone looking for the liberation of Jerusalem.

It is Luke who recounts the story about the boy Jesus when he stayed behind in Jerusalem, and the reaction of his mother, who could never forget this prophetic incident.

He describes how Martha was fussing in the kitchen while Mary sat with Jesus, spellbound by the horizons he was opening in her life.

Luke reminds us how much Jesus depended on those manifestations of human love. So Jesus is disappointed in the reaction of his fellow countrymen in Nazareth, and remarks rather sadly that a prophet never seems welcome in his own town. Jesus desires companionship.

Luke's stories abound with loving and delightful relationships that men and women share with Jesus and, through him, with one another.

In Luke, Jesus is neither "masculine" nor "feminine"; he is a fully integrated human person. He has tears in his eyes one day when he overlooks Jerusalem from a hillside in the late afternoon, listening to the noise of the traffic, mothers calling their playing children home; he complains that he would have liked to collect all the inhabitants as a mother bird gathers her brood under her wing (Lk 13:34).

He aches when he says, "The hand of the one who betrays me is with me on this table!" He is upset when, on the night of his arrest, his disciples can't keep watch with him in the garden, but continually fall asleep. He is hurt when he asks Judas, "Do you betray me with a kiss?"

Jesus is someone with deep affection for others. He loved them all so much that he could tell them, in all honesty, that his love for them would never end. Nothing would ever be able to shatter it.

It is in Luke that Jesus prays from the cross, "Father, forgive them, for they know not what they do." And addressing the thief hanging beside him, he says, "Today you will be with me in paradise" (Lk 23:34, 43).

There is nothing sentimental about this affection. When his family, including his mother, come to take him home, concerned that he has gone out of his mind, he does not rush to meet them. Instead, he points to the ones gathered around him and says, "You are all my mother, my sisters, and my brothers."

Yet he is not afraid of tenderness or intimacy. More than a dozen times Luke describes Jesus touching others or being touched by them. Luke records in Jesus a particular empathy for women.

> Christ's was not the arrogant maleness that treats women with contempt or with superior tolerance. Behind his ministry to women lay an evident *rapport* with women's thought and feeling. He really understood the frustration of the widow clamoring for a hearing by a lazy judge; the panic of a woman who had mislaid a bridal heirloom. He truly *felt* the contempt poured out upon the women in the Pharisee's house; he grieved with the desperate loss that afflicts the widow of Nain. . . . And women understood Jesus, more quickly and more deeply than did the men around him, who continued to quarrel over precedence while his heart suffered.[43]

Another characteristic of Jesus is his interest in children. He speaks about their games in the marketplace, defends them against abuse, greets them, and worries about their future. Mothers have no hesitation in bringing their children to him, and children, in turn are drawn to him. Only his male disciples protest and want to chase the children and mothers away.

Luke's writings on Jesus and the first communities are crowded with women and men who find in their relation to Jesus their own real dignity and value. In his writings no less than twenty-six women are mentioned by name.

In the Christian communities he describes, Luke discovers a tenderness, fairness, respect, love, and intimacy that are almost systematically missing in the preaching and theologies of the later church.

Bruce Wilson, an Australian theologian, has described a little exercise.[44] "First," he writes, "ask people to say what comes to their mind when they are asked to think of someone who is *very religious*." The answers Wilson usually encounters are "churchy," "rigid," "pious," "otherworldly," "judgmental," "old."

The second part of the exercise is to ask people the first thing that comes into their minds when they think of someone who could be described as *very human*. Once again the answers Wilson receives are very consistent. People will say "caring," "understanding," "warm," "kind," "forgiving," "helpful."

Wilson mentions that he has tried this project on people actually attending worship services in church. They, too, tend to give the same sort of answers as nonchurchgoers.

> But whereas non-churchgoers are matter-of-fact or "what did you expect?" about their answers, church-goers' own responses give them quite a shock. It is as though they have seen something they have never seen before. They realize that they themselves are the kind of people who would be thought "very religious." And from their knowledge about the life and teachings of the Founder of their faith, they realize that there ought not to be a split between being very religious and being a caring, understanding, warm, kind, forgiving, helpful person.[45]

Their perplexity has something to do with their attitude toward their bodies, toward their sensuality. The church in its actual clerical and religious set-up has unavoidable difficulties with human intimacy. Her official clerical leaders can hardly speak about it without getting in trouble.

Marriage has always been safeguarded by the church, but it is the celibate state that has enjoyed the greater regard. There is no doubt that the latter form of commitment, if freely and lovingly chosen, has often made priests, nuns, and lay people truly and heroically helpful and loving in their service to the larger community. It is also true that in other cases it has hardened their hearts, protected them against any form of intimacy, made them fearful of sexuality, and rendered their service void of any real love.[46]

The fact that (virtually all) Catholic priests are unmarried males has other consequences. One is that the faithful in the church are always addressed by an unmarried male clergy. It makes our church communities so different from the ones Luke describes in which women definitely played their role to the full.

Once as a youth I went to church with the most free-thinking of my uncles. He had published a number of rather liberal Catholic novels which earned him some renown. That day, the priest in the pulpit was speaking about marriage. He said that in the marital union human beings found their greatest joy and fulfillment. My uncle turned to me and said, "How does he know?"

At that time I did not understand the full impact of his question. I think he was right in a way, and at the same time he misjudged the situation. Sexuality, bodiliness, and affection often remain delicate and unresolved issues for the church. The unmarried state should not be chosen to restrict affection. It definitely would be difficult to read that intention into the life of Jesus, as depicted by Luke. Nor do we find a trace of it in his description of the lives of men and women healed and made healthy by Jesus. As R.E.O. White notes,

If Luke's contribution to the New Testament had been better appreciated, the church might have been spared the more extreme forms of asceticism which imagined some Christian virtue in the cult of dirt, hunger, vermin, flagellation, indignity, masochism, and other useless, negative, impoverishing, and life-debasing practices which Christian devotion adopted in later years.[47]

Once, during a marriage instruction session with a young couple in Nairobi, I finished by telling them they should find their delight in each other, as this was their creator's intention.

They looked at me with large wondering eyes, and some years later they wrote me to say how surprised they had been to hear such sentiments from a representative of the church! It was so un-churchy, they wrote, and when they told their friends what I had said, they, too, had been amazed. Of course they had every intention of regarding each other affectionately; but they never expected the church to encourage them!

Those of us at home in the church often seem to have a hard time being at home in our bodies. All too often we develop a negative attitude, expressed by the posture of our body in church, and the kind of furniture we tend to use.

The kneelers in the parish church of my youth were the most uncomfortable pieces of furniture I ever saw in my life. After a long service I almost always felt practically crippled. And even nowadays the pews in most churches are not much better. Knees are definitely not provided in order to sit on them!

All during my years in spiritual formation I heard the same thing: stand up straight, sit up straight, kneel properly; don't slump, don't cross your legs, walk quietly, don't run, and so forth.

During my novitiate I was introduced to certain ascetic practices: the wearing of a hair shirt (which I never did), and bracelets (spiked irons chains) you fasten around your biceps, causing quite some discomfort. I tried them for a few days but gave them up; they were too uncomfortable, which was of course their purpose.

When people hear things like that today they wonder how we could have tolerated such things in our time. Of course those same people are often fighting the natural aging of their bodies by dieting, jogging, and exercising. Perhaps asceticism has returned under a different motivation!

In the circles of missionaries after the Second Vatican Council, one of the points of discussion was the question of human development. Were missionaries called to a spiritual and sacramental apostolate only, or should they engage themselves in human development?

What did Jesus do? Did he work his miracles to heal the sick bodily because he was upset about their earthly misery, or did he work those miracles only as signs of the reality that really counted, their spiritual salvation?

The discussions were long and tedious.

In fact, they never ended, though Pope Paul VI in his encyclical *The Progress of Peoples* and John Paul II in *On Social Concern* have opted for the more integral answer. Even after we had opted for a more integrated view and began to stress the fact that human rights and the establishment of justice belong to the mission Jesus left us, we still were frequently facing the same kind of difficulty.

Jesus himself was asked the question: What is the most important remedy to introduce in our sick world? He did not answer directly that justice should be done, but that we should love God and the other as ourselves. The point is that in this way, justice cannot but be realized in an affectionate way.

And this brings us back to those swaddling clothes Mary put around the infant Jesus, whom she kissed and hugged; and to the shepherds, the stars in the night sky, Joseph, the animals, and the liberation song of Mary; and to the joy of Elizabeth, the stupor and healing of Zachariah, the astounded neighbors, the joy and delight of Simeon and Anna as they held the baby in their arms, the food and the drink, the smells and the lights, the sounds and the music, but also the dangers and risks.

The birth of Jesus shows God's trust in the future of our human life, as does the birth of any baby. Jesus' birth is a divine guarantee that we do well to continue that story in our own lives, and in the lives of our offspring.

Jesus, Emmanuel, God's incarnation among us. Here there is no hesitation, no problem. Life is assured, the future is waiting to be filled.

Mary breast-feeds her infant, who dirties his diapers like any other baby. And heaven delights! God will always be faithful to the life he gives us.

> For all existing things are dear to you and you hate nothing that you have created — why else would you have made it?
>
> How could anything have continued in existence, had it not been your will?
>
> You spare all things because they are yours, O Lord, who loves all that lives; for your imperishable breath is in every one of them. (Wisdom of Solomon 11:24–12:1)

Even should we be unfaithful to the delight for which we were originally created, God will never stop loving us. For God's imperishable breath is in each one of us, female and male, white and black, young and old, born and unborn.

This universalism is typical of Luke's approach. He traces Jesus' genealogy back to Adam (and Eve), calling him (and all of us) the Child of God (Lk 4:38b). Luke begins the Acts of the Apostles in Jerusalem and ends with Paul preaching in the streets of Rome — another demonstration of God's universal appeal.

All over the world Luke finds new spirited communities, sometimes in difficulties, but always full of hope and a sense of happiness and joy.

Ethnicity and nationality do exist, as do intrigues, but the *agape* that Jesus offers is greater than any other human bond.

Luke's story is the happiest of the four gospels. The

churches bloom and thrive. *"Things really moved around us!"* Luke writes to Theophilus, as he describes the outpouring of the Spirit of Jesus among the Parthians, Medes, Elamites, Mesopotamians, Judeans, Cappadocians, Phrygians, Egyptians, Romans, Cretans, and Arabs; sons and daughters, young and old, masters and servants, rich and poor.

It is a life program. It is the radical equality we have to live. It is the reality we have to realize. It is the tension in which we should live. It is the togetherness we have to express.

Much later this Lucan approach was lost. For centuries the Gospel of Luke was hardly considered a serious work. Scholars preferred the theological considerations of Paul and John. Luke was considered to be merely a historian, and a poor one in the bargain.

Monasticism and puritanism, world denial and male asceticism did not know what to do with him. There was too much joy, femininity, simplicity, and hope in the healing of the world in Luke.

Those old objections, which betray the mood of a pessimistic church lacking in trust in its own members, are the exact reasons why we should reread Luke in our day.

We have to grow away from any religion in which the body is the enemy of the spirit, and humanity is seen as waging a war against an antagonistic earth.

We have to liberate ourselves from any ideology that divides us against ourselves or against each other. We have to listen mercifully to ourselves, to each other, and to all the teeming yet endangered life around us.

We have to listen and to obey!

Chapter Eleven

"My Soul Magnifies the Lord!"

In the beginning of 1987 I was invited by an Australian justice and peace group to come and give a series of lectures to close the Marian year in August. I was intrigued by the invitation as I did not immediately see the relation between what this group was doing and what they expected from me. Their explanation was simple. I should have made the connection myself. Mary sung her Magnificat. Didn't that hymn tie everything together?

> My soul glorifies the Lord and my spirit rejoices in God my Savior, for he has been mindful of the humble state of his servant.
>
> From now on all generations will call me blessed, for the Mighty One has done great things for me — holy is his name.
>
> His mercy extends to those who fear him, from generation to generation.
>
> He has performed mighty deeds with his arm; he has scattered those who are proud in their inmost thoughts.
>
> He has brought down rulers from their thrones but has lifted up the humble.

He has filled the hungry with good things but has sent the rich away empty.

He has helped his servant Israel, remembering to be merciful to Abraham and his descendants forever, even as he said to our fathers. (Lk 1:46b–55)

As I thought about it, I began to see the connection between the peace and justice concerns of this Australian church group, and the song Luke put in Mary's mouth at the beginning of his Gospel.

Mary's heart must have been filled with this song. When she meets another woman, like herself carrying part of God's promise in her womb, she spontaneously bursts out with it. The song recalls ancient promises and texts — Mary must have been humming the verses to herself, even before the news of the annunciation.

Mary was someone who knew not only about the suffering of her time and age, but where the roots of the problem lay and what would have to happen to reach a solution. And that solution was going to be something more than simply giving alms! In our contemporary language, we would have to say that Mary foresaw the need for radical structural changes. If you don't believe that, read her song once more!

God was going to listen to the poor and oppressed — and their oppressors and the rich had better listen along with God!

Her call sounds like a battle hymn. It is a wave of compassion. It gives hope to all. It vibrates with the pain of everyone. Her call represents an option for the poor, the marginalized, the forgotten — because only an option for those left out of everyone else's concern is ultimately an inclusive option for everyone. For Mary realizes the truth that God truly loves us all equally.

Were this truth reflected in our world it would reverse the condition of oppression that Mary sings about. And of course, in the eyes of the rich and powerful, that sounds like a subversive message. As indeed it is.

The women who protested against Marcos in the Philippines sang this song in front of his palace. The mothers in Argentina sang it, mourning their disappeared husbands and children. Mother Teresa sang it with her sisters when they opened a hostel for AIDS patients in Washington, D.C.

What kind of person, what kind of woman was it who first sang this song? As Arturo Paoli puts it, "It is the song of one whom God has rescued from a static and pharisaic religion and put on the road to Exodus."[48] It puts Mary in the company of those groups who were formulating a religious consciousness apart from the official religious establishment of their time. Perhaps there were other like-minded women who prayed and sang these revolutionary themes in each other's company, as Mary did in her meeting with Elizabeth.

Faithful to her Jewish background, Mary nevertheless felt that one had to stretch further, one had to realize more. One had to *be* more according to the final promise and demand.

Probably all the first Christian communities looked upon themselves in similar terms. Luke mentions that the disciples continued worshiping in the temple, but at the same time introduced a new kind of organization—sharing the bread and a way of life—which complemented their Jewish practice.

The church Luke describes in Acts does not resemble the hierarchical or institutional church as we know it. In his gospel Luke never refers to "the church." He does mention "the Kingdom" thirty-eight times, but not the church. That Kingdom is a matter of living God's love for all in this world. That Kingdom is the Spirit of Jesus. Anyone can enter it.

The word "church" does appear in the Acts of the Apostles. In most cases it refers to a local community or congregation, *churches within the Church*. In three cases it seems to refer to all the congregations together: *the whole church* (Acts 8:3, 12:1, 15:22). But in no case does it refer to an organized institution.

The communities shared the same faith and welcomed each other, but were organized in different ways. Some congregations were large from the beginning, like the one in Jerusalem. Others were small. They were all composed of people who lived the radical and joyful new life of God's universal love for all, and who consequently adopted a lifestyle that contrasted with the values of their society.

It was that life that attracted Luke.

Would such a style of life be possible among us today? Is it feasible to live the Kingdom of God? Would the churches be able to join wholeheartedly in Mary's song?

The answer is not simple.

How would I answer? How would you? We are all caught in the world in which we live. We are all, in some ways, prisoners. Our society does not believe and definitely does not practice the equality of all human beings. Everyone of us knows this from our own experience. We are treated differently according to the color of our skin, the money we own, the influence we have, our affiliations, our sex, our age, and so forth.

I am writing this ten days after the United States invasion of Panama. From the first moment of that invasion we were informed about the American loss of life. But there was no mention of the bombardment of poor slum areas by the air force to make General Noriega's headquarters more accessible to American troops. Nobody knows how many Panamanians died in that bombardment. Estimates run from 330 to 1000 people burned to death in their homes. Surely, our society does not count all lives as equal.

Is there no hope for the world? Luke may have asked himself that question in the days before he heard Mary's song, before he saw with his own eyes how her prayerful battle hymn had inspired her son Jesus, his friends, and his followers, to live an alternative life.

Jesus was arrested and killed in the process, remaining absolutely faithful to his original inspiration. He simply refused to give in to the powers around him. He remained faithful to his love for others, even for the ones who killed him. *He and his love did not die.*

It is this spirit Luke finds embodied in the communities in Emmaus, in Ephesis, in Troas, in Jerusalem, in Rome, and all over his world.

He calls those groups "churches." They hang in against all that is moving their world in the way of conquest and corruption. They have an influence totally out of proportion to their numbers because they harbor in themselves the felt, but as yet unexpressed, hopes and expectations of many.

By their alternative lifestyle they give voice to the protest that is alive, but is everywhere repressed by the powers that be. They are the hope of the world.

This hope the earth needs more than ever before, for she is threatened as never before. Wherever that hope is embodied, there are the "churches"—even in the "Church."

This is not simply a possibility. It is a reality. It is happening. There are the prayer groups, the networks and communities like the Catholic Worker in the United States; the Basic Christian Communities in Latin America; the small Christian communities in Africa; the lay communities and movements that are forming all over Europe; the peace and justice groups in Asia; international, ecumenical and interreligious communities engaging in common worship, dialogue, and development work; societies and congregations that are opening their doors to accept associate members, and so on.

And wherever this happens, this risen life attracts the attention of the modern-day Lukes of our time. It is the work of the Spirit, who cannot be bound.

Epilogue

Loosening the Bonds

In the beginning of this book we asked a question: Why remain faithful to the church? The answer has not proved simple; indeed, it has many layers.

In Luke's Gospel Jesus tells us that the Kingdom of God is within us. Luke says the same thing when he tells us that the Spirit of Jesus is with us. That Spirit is not only with you, or with me; it is with *us*.

We are not only loved by our Creator; we share in our Creator's love. God's love is our life.

It is not difficult to see that we do not live up to that standard. Listening to the poor and the wretched, listening to their sighs of anxiety and fear, we need little proof of how far we fall short. But if we listen, we can't prevent those cries from leaving a lasting echo within us.

Listening and "obeying" what we hear is not an easy task. It is even more difficult to analyze and unmask the structures in our world that are the underlying causes of the existing injustices and lack of love. Such an analysis is a process of "conscientization," as they say in Latin America. Such an analysis is itself a threat to the existing order and it will be taken as a form of criticism. It puts us in the camp of the "enemy."

Until recently, such criticism was called reactionary and

capitalist in the East, while in the West it was called Marxist or communist. As the world changes, the names may change. But a threat will always remain a threat, regardless of the prevailing ideology.

The first one in Luke's writings who gives a clear sign of having listened to the cry of the poor and the sighs of her own heart is Mary.

Singing her battle hymn she brings her son into this world; and he, in turn, learns to sing his mother's song. Like her, he begins to lean against the existing world around him: Things must change!

Jesus lived God's love among us. It was joy to be in his company. He was a delight, sincerely sharing, obediently listening to the misery around him, and affectionately loving all those with whom he came in contact.

After he left his disciples, they came together in communities Luke calls "churches." It is in one of those communities that Luke first meets the Spirit of Jesus. Immediately he recognizes it from within his own as yet unexpressed hopes and desires. He *remembers* the future!

Not that everything in those communities is ideal. There are constant difficulties in the sharing of their property (Acts 5:1–10), and there is discrimination in such simple things as the distribution of soup (Acts 6:1–2). Again and again the communities fall short of their promises. And each time the Kingdom horizon beckons them on.

The result is a tension. The communities enlarge their plans, they expand their horizons, they widen their tables. But every time they do, at the moment when their new projects are realized, another woman like Mary, with a son like Jesus, says no, this is not yet as it should be.

Once again a group begins leaning in against what seems to be settled and established.

The church offers an answer, but at the same time that answer can become a wall that has to be broken through.

The church is like a child reaching for the moon. The child

can't reach it from her bed, so she says, "If I get out of bed and open the window and stretch my hand as far as I can, then I will be able to touch it." And when that doesn't work: "If I climb on the roof I will be able to get at it." And later: "Gosh, no again. . . . But maybe if I climb in the church tower I will succeed. . . ." But even the highest church tower is not high enough.

This analogy is not completely correct. In its sacramental signs and models the church does touch and realize its vision. But even that is only true up to a point.

Our liturgy and worship do not exclusively center on God's equal love for all. They center only on a group. Old outdated discriminations of gender and color, of age and influence, of history and tradition, of religious allegiances and political ideologies keep the churches apart. Not only are our churches divided against each other, but we ourselves in the church are divided over classes and ranks. Discussions on the distribution of power and influence, the order of precedence and other such issues has never stopped, though Jesus had sharp words for the whole subject: Among you, it should not be like that; there should be no longer any first or last.

Liberation theology, feminist theology, creation-centered theologies — each in their way are reactions against the limits the church's actualized visions impose on us.

Those limits also account for the existence of so many prayer groups, peace and justice networks, para-liturgies, agape celebrations, meditation circles, small communities, and Bible discussion groups. Not to mention all those who are organizing themselves in religious movements and tendencies under the heading of New Age religion: channeling, transcendental meditation, dream interpretation, community living, yoga, and so forth.

Humanity's problem is not that we are no longer religious.

The issue seems to be that we are *too* religious for the way our religious needs are met in some of our so-called religious institutions.

Caught in the old but still very vigorous structures of the world, these institutions cannot offer the fulfillment, comfort, and security we are looking for. We are greater than this world; but also greater than the church.

It would be nice to think that what we are looking for might be available in some quick fix. But there is no quick fix.

What we are looking for is hiding beyond ourselves, beyond our world. We are hoping for wholeness. We are striving after the real.

Being with the Spirit of Jesus connects us intimately not only with each other and the whole of creation; it situates us in the life of divinity itself.

Luke does not elaborate on this theme. But it appears in the work of a later author. The author of the Gospel of John reflects on how the whole of creation is created in God's offspring, the Son. *Creation is in a sense the face of that Son, Christ.*

We can discover something of this in ourselves, in others, in the world around us. It is a broken face, a fragmented one, yet everywhere believers and nonbelievers, mystics and counselors, are bringing the pieces together.

We have never seen the whole of the face, as yet. But we begin to intuit better and better that it all fits together: the young and the old, the sky and the water, the tropical forests and the oxygen we need, the birds and the grass, the plants and trees given for the healing of the nations, the rich and the poor.

It is as if we all begin to remember that we once saw the whole face, long, long ago.

The same John who saw the whole of reality created in God's offspring, in the beginning of his Gospel, also described the dramatic coming together of the whole of nature and the gathering of all the nations in the last book of the Christian Bible, the Book of Revelation.

Being created in God's offspring we are taken up in the life of the Trinity. It is in that mystery that the mystery about ourselves is hidden.

It is a mystery we express every time someone is initiated into it: in the name of the Father, the Son, and the Holy Spirit—the Source, the Offspring, and the Life.

We are accustomed to symbolizing the relation of these three by the triangle. It would be better to think of a circle in which—as an ancient Church tradition has it—the three are dancing and caroling in their celebration of life.[49]

A triangle suggests a top and a bottom.

A circle dance does not. In the twirl of the dance there might be three but no first, second, or third.

Dancing I remain one, and my partner is another. But in the dance this separation seems to flow away: am I the dancer, am I my partner, is my partner me, or are *we* both the dance?

We are invited to dance with *Them* in love. As the old hymn suggests: Jesus is the *Lord of the Dance* among us.

The actual church remains an answer to this divine invitation. She is an answer. She is an answer that falls short. The church is not the Kingdom.

The church is an answer that can become rigid and stiff. It is an answer that does not go far enough, just as we ourselves are not going far enough and are hesitant to dance as we should with the people and the world around us.

The church cannot but fall short of the promise of the Kingdom we all carry in our hearts.

Mary, too, carried that promise when she sang her battle hymn. That promise made her defy the religious and secular institutions of her time.

It is that promise that keeps the People of God on their way, continuing on in the direction that was chosen long ago, and realizing better from day to day what being loved by God means for us and for the world around us.

We have to free ourselves and the church from the old ways that hinder our pilgrimage. Joining the churches within the Church, according to our own charisms and gifts, letting the Spirit of Jesus in us join that Spirit in others, penetrating the whole of the world in Jesus—it is there that our hope and salvation lie.

Arturo Paoli says it well:

> But here and there signs appear, little breakthroughs of *a hidden church within the Church*. ... These break-throughs are enough to give me hope and the courage needed to continue the struggle for the entry of the whole church into the perspective of Mary.[50]

That is the answer I would have liked to give every time those questions, "Why remain faithful to the church? Why remain fascinated by Jesus?" were asked of me.

It is not the answer I have always given. It is the answer I do give now. It is the answer I suggest to you. It is the answer I give myself.

The struggle continues. It continues until our hands are taken by one who reaches from far away, and from deep within, to draw us into the dance, together, from here unto eternity.

Now and then in liberating moments, the dance breaks through in our lives, breakthroughs of the new and resurrected human life Luke encountered in the early Christian communities. He encountered people enlivened by the Spirit of Jesus—not only faithful to the eucharistic breaking of the bread, but agents of the Kingdom of God sought and realized. Luke is referring to those events and realizations when he writes about "the things that *have been accomplished among us*" (Lk 1:1).

Luke's reports are full of the enthusiasm and joy of the communities, their inventive courage, their social and constructive care, and their creative idealism—all attitudes as badly needed in our time as they were in the ancient world. As Luke notes, people held Christians in high esteem, and nevertheless did not dare to join them (Acts 5:13). The new life must have seemed to them too great a threat to the life they were accustomed to. Yet, in the next sentence Luke reports that multitudes of men and women did join them (Acts 5:14). Afraid for the new, worrying about the old, they nevertheless overcame their fears and joined. The new life offered too much that was unmistakably divine and genuinely human.

I wish that we might develop again a Christian lifestyle that would represent that kind of threat to all that is evil and harmful in this world, while yet, at the same time, offering such a source of blessing and healing: a life that would be a real alternative.

Luke's point to Theophilus is that it can be done. He saw it with his own eyes. The promise, the power, and the glory are all given. It is up to us to get our act together, to reorient our lives and live the Spirit of Jesus given to us. We have to come together to organize the old anew.

Notes

1. Robert Blair Kaiser, *The Politics of Sex and Religion* (Kansas City: Leaven Press, 1985), p. 15.
2. See Grace Jantzen, "The Mystic as Subversive," *The Tablet*, June 24, 1989, p. 725.
3. Dr. John Dominian, "Spirituality in the West" (unpublished paper; June 1988), p. 7.
4. *The Washington Post*, December 23, 1989, p. C12.
5. *The Sunday Times* (London), December 24, 1989, p. A3.
6. R.E.O. White, *Luke's Case for Christianity* (London: The Bible Reading Fellowship, 1987), p. 19.
7. Jan Grootaers, "The Laity within the Ecclesial Community," Pro Mundi Vita, Bulletin 106, no. 3, 1986, p. 6.
8. Cf. J.A. Jungmann, *De Lois de la Célébration Liturgique* (Paris: 1956), p. 38f.
9. Grootaers, "The Laity," p. 5.
10. Cf. Avery Dulles, S.J., "Introduction to the Dogmatic Constitution on the Church (*Lumen Gentium*)," in Walter M. Abbott, S.J., ed., *The Documents of Vatican II* (New York: Guild Press, 1966), pp. 9-13.
11. White, *Luke's Case*, p. 109.
12. Marcello deC. Azevedo, *Basic Ecclesial Communities* (Washington, D.C.: Georgetown University Press, 1987), p. 140.
13. Quoted in *AFER* (Eldoret, Kenya), October 1976, pp. 266f.
14. R. Luneau, *Laisse Aller Mon Peuple* (Paris: Karthala, 1987), p. 40.
15. Jan Grootaers, "Laity in the Field: Polarities and Convergences," Pro Mundi Vita, Bulletin 110, no. 3, 1987, p. 26.
16. For a good idea of the methods used, see Anne Hope and Sally Timmel, *Training for Transformation: A Handbook for Community Workers*, vols. I-III (Gweru, Zimbabwe: Mambo Press, 1984).
17. Cf. *Origins* vol. 18, no. 35 (February 9, 1989), pp. 561-95.

18. *Origins* vol. 18, no. 42 (March 30, 1989), p. 699.

19. William E. Phipps, "Jesus the Prophetic Pharisee," *Journal of Ecumenical Studies* vol. 14, no. 1 (Winter 1977), p. 30.

20. Stuart Rosenberg, "Contemporary Renewal and the Jewish Experience," paper delivered to the 1968 International Conference of Christians and Jews, York University, Toronto, Canada, September 1968, p. 4. Quoted in John T. Pawlikowski, *Christ in the Light of the Christian-Jewish Dialogue* (New York: Paulist Press, 1982), p. 85.

21. Pawlikowski, pp. 103f.

22. Dominian, "Spirituality in the West," pp. 12f.

23. *The Road Less Traveled* (New York: Simon & Schuster, 1978).

24. Andrew M. Greeley, *Happy Are Those Who Thirst for Justice* (New York: Warner Books, 1987), pp. viii-ix.

25. Peck, *Road Less Traveled By*, p. 120.

26. See my report on this in *Non-Bourgeois Theology* (Maryknoll, N.Y.: Orbis Books, 1985).

27. London: SPCK, 1979.

28. Ibid., pp. 24f.

29. Aloysius Pieris, "The Religious Vows and the Reign of God," *The Way*, Supplement 65, Summer 1989, p. 7

30. Zygmunt Bauman, quoted in Istvan Deak, "The Incomprehensible Holocaust," *New York Review of Books*, XXXVI:14 (September 28, 1989), p. 72. Italics mine.

31. Pieris, "The Religious Vows," p. 5.

32. For further information on this community see Elizabeth O'Connor, *Call to Commitment* (New York: Harper and Row, 1983; first ed., 1963).

33. Pope John Paul II, *On Social Concern* (Washington, D.C.: U.S. Catholic Conference, 1987), n. 42.

34. Pope Paul VI, *The Progress of Peoples* (Washington, D.C.: U.S. Catholic Conference, 1967).

35. David Morris, "Recycling is not Enough," *Building Economic Alternatives*, a quarterly publication of Co-op America, Winter 1989, p. 4.

36. Alex Levin, "Recycle: Do the Right Thing," *Building Economic Alternatives*, ibid, p. 8.

37. Tom McGrath, "A Rude Awakening for Sleeping Beauties?," *Salt*, January 1990, p. 25.

38. David B. Barrett, "Silver and Gold Have I None: Church of the Poor or Church of the Rich?," *International Bulletin of Missionary Research*, vol. 7, n. 4, October 1983, p. 148.

39. John S. Pobee, *Who Are the Poor? The Beatitudes as a Call to Community* (Geneva: World Council of Churches Publications, 1987), p. 68.

40. Dominian, "Spirituality in the West," p. 15.

41. Pieris, "Religious Vows," p. 7.

42. Elie Wiesel, *Night* (London: Collins, 1981), p. 76.

43. White, "Luke's Case," pp. 96f.

44. Bruce Wilson, *Ten Gods Survive in Australia?* Sutherland, Australia: Albatross Books, 1983.

45. Ibid., 160.

46. Ibid.

47. White, p. 106.

48. Arturo Paoli, *Meditations on Saint Luke* (Maryknoll, N.Y.: Orbis Books, 1977), p. 190.

49. See. Leonardo Boff, *Trinity and Society* (Maryknoll, N.Y.: Orbis Books, 1988).

50. Paoli, p. 114.

JOHN E. COCKAYNE, JR.